Forex Trading Simple Strategies

All You Need to Know to Start Trading Forex and Learn Successful Strategies With a Quick Daily Routine for Beginners to Make Money for a Living

Matthew Bear

Table of Contents

Introduction 1
Chapter 1: What is Forex 4
    Forex Defined 4
    What is the Forex Market 5
    Can Forex Trading Be a Full-Time Business 6
    Where Did Forex Come From 8
    Understanding FX Dealers 9
    How Is Forex Different, and Why Trade on Forex 10
    The Forex Market is Huge 12
    Forex Has Massive Leverage 13
    Forex vs. Crypto 14
    Next Steps 15
Chapter 2: Opening a Trading Account 16
    Things to Look for When Selecting an FX Dealer 16
    How to Open a Forex Trading Account 18
    When Can You Begin Trading 20
    Some Well-Known FX dealers 20
    Spreads 24
    Summary: What to Look for When Choosing a Dealer 24
    What's Next 25
Chapter 3: Currency Pairs and PIPS 26
    Currency Pair Trading 26
    The Majors 29
    Summary: How Currency Pairs Work 33
    PIPS 36
    Japanese Yen 37
    How Traders Talk About Pips 39
    Price Quotes, Spread, Buying, and Selling 40
    Buying and Selling 42
    SWAPS 45

Chapter 4: PIPS, Micros, Minis, and Standard Lots 48

Lot Sizes Used When Trading Currency 48
Price Per Pip 49
Micro Lot 49
Mini Lot 49
Standard Lot 50
Number of Lots and Pip Moves 51
Account Sizes 53
How Will Different Pip Moves Impact Your Account 53
Understanding Pips and Charts 54
Currency Units Explained 58
How to Start Your Trading 58
Position Sizes 59
How to Figure the Amount of Cash You Need to Enter a Trade ... 60
Understanding Trade Size Using Volume 63
Your Account and Margin 64

Chapter 5: Understanding Charts 65

Remember What the Chart Is Charting 65
What Is a candlestick 67
Structure of a Candlestick 69
Reversal Signals 71
    Bullish Reversal Signals 71
    Bearish Candlestick Patterns 76
    Candlestick Patterns – The Bottom Line 78
Moving Averages 78
Drawing Trend lines 82

Chapter 6: Forex Trading Strategies 84

Swing Trading 86
Scalping 90
Intraday Trading 92
Position Trading 93
News Traders 93
Trend trading 94
End of Day Trading 94

Chapter 7: Forex Trading Strategies – Techniques 96
Trendline Trading 96
CCI Moving Average Strategy 97
Bollinger Band Trading Strategy 97
Gartley Fibonacci Patterns 98
The Floor Trader Strategy 99
SuperTrends 100
Hull Moving Average 101
Which Daily Routine Strategies to Use 103

Chapter 8: Tips, Tricks, and Mistakes to Avoid 107
Train on a Demo Platform 108
Having a Trading Plan 110
Trading Emotions 114

Conclusion 115

Introduction

If you've been looking into different ways to invest your money, there is no doubt that you've come across lots of talk about FOREX. In fact, it's probably the most popular investing topic out there when it comes to traders, more popular than options trading, more popular than day trading, and more popular than swing trading.

Why all the hype?

As we'll see, FOREX has many things going for it. Compared to all the trading methods we've mentioned, it's the new kid on the block. FOREX trading only became available to small, individual investors during the past 20 years.

First of all, what is FOREX? Just to be clear in case some readers aren't quite sure what it's about, the word "Forex" is shorthand for foreign exchange. This is a global market where currencies are traded against one another. So it's where dollars are traded against pounds, or Euros are traded against Japanese Yen.

Since you have to trade one currency for another, they are always traded against one another. If you are trading Great British Pounds against Euros, then you are either buying Euros with Great British Pounds (therefore betting on the Euro to rise in value, relative to the Great British Pound), or you are buying Great British Pounds with Euros (betting that Pounds will rise in value relative to the Euro).

As we'll see, this is a great way for small investors like yourself to make a profit. However, trading on Forex is a little bit tricky, so you shouldn't get involved with trading until you've thoroughly educated yourself. You need to understand what Forex really is, how it works, and what your trades really mean. You'll also need to know how to get into trades and why to get into trades, and the many strategies that have been developed over the past 20 years to ensure that you can have some level of trading success.

For those that are willing to put in the hard work, which not only means trading smart but also educating yourself and studying Forex, this can be a lucrative way to earn profits. And it's a lot of fun too.

Let's quickly review what you're going to get out of this book. First, we are going to introduce the Forex market and quickly explain what it's all about and its history. We will also explain the why of Forex, in other words, the reasons why you might want to trade on Forex rather than with other financial securities. Then we'll explain the technical details so that you can understand how to read the information coming out of the markets and know what it means, be able to accurately enter trades, and know how much you are gaining or losing.

Then we'll talk about choosing a broker. It's always important to get off on the right foot, and having the best broker is a large part of that process.

With the foundations out of the way, we will begin discussing the "tools of the trade." You'll learn how to apply fundamental and technical analysis in order to determine when to enter and exit trades, to get the best odds on earning profits.

Then we'll talk about the mentality and best practices to use with Forex trading. There are many important things to learn about Forex trading, if you've never done it before. If you've had some previous experience trading options or stocks, that will be really helpful, but trading Forex has its own nuances that you need to become familiar with. People who are new to trading will need to learn what it's like to be in the daily pressure cooker and how to deal with it.

Finally, we'll talk about managing risks and developing a winning trading plan, and give some tips on success with Forex trading.

Forex trading involves putting real money at risk, but that said I hope you're ready to have some fun too! Forex trading can be fun, interesting, and also lucrative. Let's get started on your journey to success!

Chapter 1: What is Forex

Before we explore trading strategies that will increase the odds of profit, it's important to have a solid understanding of what the Forex market is all about and how it works. A large part of that is getting to know where the Forex market came from and how it's developed through the years. From there, it's important to get a handle on how Forex trading works in practice and how it's different than other markets.

Forex Defined

As we noted in the introduction, Forex means *foreign exchange*. This is a market where the world's currencies are traded against one another, which determines the exchange rates that are used worldwide when converting from one currency to another. This type of currency conversion happens all the time, countless times every single day.

If you are traveling, you'll find yourself having to change dollars for Mexican Pesos, or Euros for Great British Pounds. A business importing parts from Japan will create a situation where dollars have to be converted into Japanese Yen at some point. In order to use their revenues in their home country, the Japanese company will need to trade the dollars they receive for Yen.

The rates that are used for transactions like these are set on the Forex market. Like stock market prices, the exchange rates between currencies are constantly fluctuating. One day, the dollar might be favored against the Euro, but the next day, it might be the other way around.

What is the Forex Market

The Forex market is a bit different than the stock market, if you are thinking in those terms. The first thing to note is that the Forex market is completely global. There is Forex trading in New York, London, Singapore, and Sydney. Since the trading that is taking place is global, the Forex markets are open 24 hours a day on business days.

This is exciting for small investors because starting Sunday evening when the markets in New Zealand open, you can begin trading 24 hours a day until the weekend arrives the following Friday afternoon. Understanding the impact of the many different trading centers is important, the times of transition can impact trading volume and other factors. For example, if you are trading in the United States, you'll want to be paying attention when the trading day in New York is winding down, but trading in London is starting to get going.

The Forex market isn't only global; it's not really like NASDAQ or the New York Stock Exchange. You can think of Forex as being an over the counter market. It's very fast-paced, and that can be exciting for many people but stressful for others. But as there are many different trading styles that work on the stock markets, there are many different trading styles that work on Forex. You can be a day trader on Forex, or you can swing trade. Or you could hold a position over a long time period. There are many different ways to go about trading on Forex in order to make profits.

But there are many strategies that are unique to Forex, that result from the unique properties of the market and the assets being traded, and how they are being traded. We will be discussing those throughout the book, so that you can figure out the style that would be the best fit for your personality and level of pressure and risk you are willing to accept. There are also many different styles of trading that can be adjusted, depending on the time commitment that you are willing or able to put into your trading.

Can Forex Trading Be a Full-Time Business

Let's face it; many of us hate our "day jobs." As a result, lots of people come to Forex hoping to either strike it rich or to at least be able to quit their day job. Markets are fun and interesting, and so lots of people would rather spend their "working" time focusing on finance and making trades, as opposed to slaving away at a desk for someone else.

But the question is, how realistic is it to make a living doing this? I'll be honest with you: many Forex traders end up failing. However, it's definitely possible to make a living trading Forex and it's also possible to make a large sum of money doing it, although the proportion of people that make millions is relatively small.

The fact is, the reason that lots of people fail at Forex trading is that they take a casual approach to it that isn't going to work. They just start trading on a whim without actually putting the time in to study and learn how it really works.

The second factor that causes people to fail is that they let emotion take over their trading. When you have real money on the line, it's only natural to feel emotions like panic, or elation and even greed. But letting emotions take over your trading is a recipe for disaster. Those who are able to trade as if they were "Mr. Spock" are the traders who become profitable. I am warning you right from the get-go, if you let emotion rule your trades you will fail to make profits. We will talk about some tips and explore the trading mindset so that you can avoid falling prey to this common problem.

Third, reckless trading practices like risking your entire account on one trade lead many people to fail. We will talk about good trading practices and how to minimize risk later in the book. We will also explore ways to create a trading plan. Just like with emotion, people who create a trading plan are the ones who are able to make a living trading on Forex, those who trade on a whim or a series of whims either find themselves losing money, or merely breaking even. To be blunt, the choice is yours from this moment forward. All I can do is give you the advice; it's going to be up to you in order to get it done.

If you don't fall prey to the top reasons for failure, then making a full-time living trading on Forex markets is a real possibility, even likelihood. Once you get established, then it's only a matter of consistently growing to earn profits.

Where Did Forex Come From

If you are under the age of 40, you probably feel like there has always been a Forex market. If you are over 40, then it probably seems like it came out of nowhere. So what is the story behind this?

Prior to the late 1990s, the currency exchange was very different. Basically, the currency exchange was not available to small investors. Back in the old days, currency exchange only went on between the big banks and large "smart money" players that were allowed in on the action. That was a very different world, and compared to today's Forex markets; it was slow and lumbering. This is called interbank trading. Transactions were settled at the end of each day, which is completely different from the way it works today.

The 1990s was an explosive decade. The internet was "invented," and this opened up a lot of opportunities for business and investing. Some smart people got together in the mid-to-late 1990s and saw an opportunity to open up Forex trading to the general public.

What they came up with was a system that set up an intermediary between the banks and the general public, using something like a middle man broker. The broker would trade with the banks, and then they would turn around and make trades with individuals. This is how the modern Forex market was born, and it's how it was opened up to individuals like us to get involved.

The intermediary or middle man between the banks and the public is called a Forex dealer, or FX Dealer for short.

Interbank trading still goes on, but trading using FX dealers had exploded since 1998, when the first dealer began operating. The way it works is pretty simple. Banks and FX dealers trade with one another. The liquidity in the system is provided by the big banks. The FX dealers then trade with small and individual traders among the general public.

Understanding FX Dealers

It's important to know this as background information, but when you actually begin trading, it won't be all that important. In any case, it's actually pretty easy to understand, so let's have a deeper look at how the system works behind the scenes.

As we said, an FX dealer trades with the banks and also with the general public. There are different types of FX dealers. One type of FX dealer is called a dealing desk. The fundamental point of the dealing desk is that the dealing desk takes the other side of the trade. So if you opt to buy Euros with US Dollars, the dealing desk sells you the Euros. In the early days, this was a conflict of interest, but in today's markets, this runs very smoothly and fairly, and there are other types of dealers as well.

The other type is called straight-through processing, or STP. This is an FX dealer that operates more like a stock brokerage. That is, when you put in a trade, an STP dealer finds another trader to take the other side of the position. That can be an individual trader, or it could even be a bank. But the dealer themselves do not take the other side of the trade.

As the markets have evolved, the price differences between the two methods have become minimal to non-existent. So you shouldn't be concerned about any conflict of interest in doing business with a dealing desk, the trade is going to be the same either way as far as practical matters are concerned.

Typically, large trades don't work well with an STP. We are talking about trades on the order of a million dollars per trade and up. Those large trades are going to go through a dealing desk, because finding an individual trader willing to take the trade would be a time-consuming process. In order to keep the market liquid and running smoothly, running large trades like that through a dealing desk makes sense. Think of it as the "market maker" on the options markets, who will take the other side of a trade, if necessary, to keep the markets liquid and smooth.

Small trades (which can seem quite large to us individual investors) work well with STP forex dealers. So chances are this is what you're going to be dealing with, if you are trading less than a million dollars per trade. If you are trading hundreds or thousands of dollars at a time, my bet is you're more than likely dealing with STP, and another individual is taking the other side of the trade.

We will talk about opening an account and brokers in the next chapter.

How Is Forex Different, and Why Trade on Forex

One of the first things that new traders need to wrap their minds around is that Forex is a bit of a different animal than they are used to. First, let's consider stocks. When you trade on the stock market, you basically buy shares of stock and hope that the price goes up. Well, let me be it a bit careful about my language here, you shouldn't be "hoping" for a price increase. Hopefully, you are going to do your homework, and so there is a probability of a price increase, so that you have a reasonable chance of earning profits off coming price moves. There are many ways to trade to earn profits off price movements; day traders will look to make their profits in a single day or even over the course of hours, often trading in highly volatile penny stocks. Swing traders hope to take advantage of "price swings" that last from days to even months.

Other people are long-term investors, and they put their money in a company for the long haul, maybe over a period of 10-30 years. They are riding the long-term growth of the company and working to build a retirement fund. Investors of this type often look for stable, dividend-paying stocks in order to earn an income off their investments.

Big players with margin accounts will also short stock, which means they profit on stock market declines. The way this works is they borrow shares using their margin account, and they sell them on the open market when the price is still relatively high. Then they wait for the price to collapse, and buy the shares back at a lower price. They return the borrowed shares to the broker and pocket the difference.

There is one key point in all of this. When you are investing in stocks, options, or mutual funds, you are investing in *one* financial security. The same holds for gold, silver, or oil and gas futures.

When you invest in Amazon, no matter your trading style, you aren't trading Amazon against Netflix. Imagine how different the stock market would be if instead of trading one individual company, you invested in the relative difference between Amazon and Netflix.

On currency markets, that is basically what you do. Each currency trades against all other currencies, and you are betting on the rise or fall of that currency against another currency, when you make a trade. If you buy Euros with dollars, then you are betting on the Euro rising in price with respect to the dollar, and you're shorting the dollar, essentially. If your bet goes right, when you close your trade, you'll be able to get more dollars back than you put in, which will be more valuable at home, if you live in the United States.

You can also make independent bets on either currency, so you can buy Japanese Yen or Mexican Pesos with Euros.

Currencies always trade in *pairs*. Individual currencies are not the central thing on the Forex markets; currency pairs are. That is the first thing to wrap your mind around when learning about how the Forex markets work. It's not anything that is too difficult to understand, but it is a different way of thinking that most people are not used to, since they have been exposed to trading and investment through the stock markets.

The Forex Market is Huge

The second thing about the Forex market that you can learn about for your fundamental education is that the trading volume on Forex markets is absolutely massive. About $170-$200 billion is traded on the New York Stock Exchange daily. That is certainly nothing to sneeze at; it's big money.

However, in the Forex markets, some $5 trillion changes hand every single day. In part, this is due to the fact that the market is global. It's also simply because Forex markets have attracted a huge amount of interest.

That huge amount of trading volume and cash has practical implications. In short, it means the market is highly liquid. You can get into and exit your trades quickly. Think about the implications of a worldwide market, if you are taking one side of a trade, finding someone to take the other side of a trade is not something that's difficult to do.

Compared to options trading, this can be important. Many companies only have a small interest in their options, and so if you trade their options and need to get out of them fast, it can be difficult closing a deal. That can mean lost profits, or if it's a losing trade that can mean that you might face larger losses than you would have, if the market for that option were more liquid.

Forex Has Massive Leverage

Another difference between Forex and other types of trading is that you can get huge amounts of leverage on Forex markets. In some countries, you can get 100 to 1 leverage, in the United States, it's 50 to 1. It's expected that countries like the UK, Canada, and Australia will be moving to the rule used in the United States, if they haven't already, but even 50 to 1 leverage is just incredible.

Compare this to a typical margin account with stocks. In that case, you get 2 to 1 leverage.

Let's explain what this means, in case there are some readers who don't understand the concept. If you have an account with 2 to 1 leverage, then if you put $2,000 cash on the trade, you could buy $4,000 worth of stock.

So on the currency markets, its 50 to 1 in the United States. So that means that if you put in $100 cash, you could enter a trade of $5,000. That is an amazing expansion of your buying power.

It's important to understand that leverage cuts both ways. One problem that can arise with new traders is that they become blinded to the possibilities, and they only think in terms of making money. But you can lose money too. While leverage can magnify your winning trades, it can magnify your losing trades as well. And you don't want to get in a situation where you owe a broker a lot of money, or you wipe out your account. That is a real possibility when trading, so you cannot be careless when using leverage.

Forex vs. Crypto

Crypto is the next big thing. It's hard to say how it's going to play out; the world's governments are not taking a liking to crypto. But let's leave that aside for a moment and just talk briefly about the differences between crypto and Forex.

First off, with crypto, it's not a real currency. I would liken trading crypto to buying tulip bulbs until you can use crypto to purchase hard assets on the wider market. Facebook is attempting to do this with their Libra currency, but it looks like several governments might actually put a stop to Facebook's plans. Until you can trade crypto for a hard asset like a house or car, you're only hoping that the price of crypto is going to keep increasing. Do your research on the tulip bulb craze, if you don't know what that is. This has happened before.

On Forex, you are investing in a real financial asset with real value – that is, any world currency can be exchanged for hard financial assets, stocks, gold, etc. The currencies are backed by the government.

Second, as I mentioned, if you put money into bitcoin, you are simply hoping that bitcoin is going to increase in value as its bid up. Forex doesn't work that way; as we mentioned earlier, you are investing in one currency against another.

The hope of crypto is to get a currency that is independent of government control. That may or may not be a noble goal depending on your perspective, but one risk for crypto in the coming years is that if governments are actively working against it, merchants are going to be unwilling to accept it in exchange for real goods and services. That is going to put crypto squarely in the tulip bulb category.

We don't know how things are going to play out, crypto might be the wave of the future, but when you have all the worlds governments against you that is not a point in its favor.

Next Steps

Well, this is the basic foundation of Forex. Now you know how the modern version of the market came to be, and some of the basic differences between Forex trading versus other types of financial securities. In the next chapter, we will explore the process of choosing a broker and opening your first account so that you can actually start trading.

Chapter 2: Opening a Trading Account

The first thing to do in order to get started, besides educating yourself on how to trade, is to open a trading or brokerage account. In many ways, this isn't too different from opening a stock trading account, and so it will be somewhat familiar to many readers. In fact, some of the most famous brokerages also allow you to open a Forex trading account.

Things to Look for When Selecting an FX Dealer

The first thing that I would consider if I were opening a new account is how experienced the dealer was. I would be less interested in opening an account with a brand-new dealer. The dealer may be legitimate, but you are taking a chance of opening an account with someone who does not have a proven history. That was worth the gamble in the early days of Forex trading, but after 20 years the market is in a more mature phase, and so there really isn't any reason to be taking chances.

So, the first thing to consider is the length of time that the dealer has been in business. I would opt for at least five years of history, but you can shop around and find varying amounts of time in business. A longer time frame that the company has been in business means that the company is established and therefore is generally speaking, more trustworthy.

If a long time, the established brokerage has recently entered the Forex arena, that might be an exception. If the company is a well known and experienced stock brokerage, then you know that this is a well established and reliable business. They can be trusted to conduct honest trades, they are going to be upfront about their fees, and they are going to be trustworthy handling your financials.

Think about that for a moment. When you are opening a trading account, you are possibly trusting someone to handle hundreds, thousands, tens of thousands, and even more dollars of your hard-earned money. You don't want to be sending that kind of money to a fly by night operation in the Bahamas or Nigeria, when we are talking about trading and investing.

This can be problematic because these days it's pretty easy to set up a nice-looking website. Someone in their mother's basement with a computer can create a website in a few minutes that will look completely professional and established. So, the appearances put out by a company are less important than any hard data that you can come across, with respect to the company.

One piece of advice is to only go with brokerages and FX dealers that are regulated and audited. There are some countries that you can guarantee that this is the case and many countries where you cannot be sure. Generally speaking, the following countries are solid for this purpose: the United States, the United Kingdom, Canada, Australia, New Zealand, and Singapore. Hong Kong and Japan are also stable, regulated marketplaces. FX dealers in these countries are regulated and audited on a regular basis, so that you can rest easy at night knowing that your money is being kept safe, and that you are not going to be cheated when making trades.

How to Open a Forex Trading Account

In some ways, opening a Forex trading account can be a little bit more complicated than opening a stock market account. The main reason is that Forex offers some opportunities for money laundering and other activities. As a result, a legitimate broker is going to be putting a little more effort into verifying your identity. Let's take a look at some of the steps involved in this process.

Typically, when you open a stock trading account in your home country, all you have to do is link a bank account and provide some basic information. When you open an account with an FX dealer, this is going to involve a few extra steps. It might take a little bit of time, but in the end, it will be no big deal. In a nutshell, legitimate FX dealers are required to verify that you are who you say you are, and that you are a citizen and so forth. So what are the steps involved in the verification process?

The first is that you have to apply to open a trading account. This is a simple process that is done online. So, it will be familiar to anyone who has applied for a credit card or anything else online. You will have to answer some simple questions about your identity, place of residence, and other basic information.

Then you are going to be required to provide documentation that the dealer uses to prove your identity, in order to fight money laundering. You are going to have to prove that you are a citizen of the country, and you will also need to provide some proof of residence. In the United States, sending a copy of your driver's license is probably going to be adequate, in order to verify your citizenship. I live in the United States so cannot give details on proving citizenship in other countries, please check with your local brokerage for more information.

You should open a brokerage in your home country if you live in one of the countries aforementioned. Remember that you can trade 24 hours a day in any market, whether the trading is currently happening in Tokyo or London won't matter to you. So you don't need to open an account in the UK to trade during UK hours.

In the United States, proof of residence may vary by broker, but the kinds of things that brokers are going to be interested in using could include a copy of a bank statement that has your name and address on it, or possibly a copy of a utility bill that has your name and address on it. Consequently, it is really not a big deal to verify your identity and get the account opened.

However, someone needs to go over and verify the documents, so don't get too anxious. It will take between one and two days, in most cases, to verify your identity and approve the application. Once the application is approved, you are ready to get started.

The next step after application approval is to fund your account. Once we get to this step, there is literally no difference between a stock market account with a brokerage and an account with a Forex dealer.

You will enter your bank account information and then initiate a wire transfer to fund your account with the FX dealer. The amount of time required for this may vary from dealer to dealer, but typically this is a very fast process, once your account has been approved for trading. It may also depend on your bank as well, but in many cases, you will have your account funded very quickly.

Make sure that you have the funds in your bank. I know that should go without saying, but be aware that some brokers will credit your account, before the wire transfer is actually completed. You don't want to get off on the wrong foot with a broker by having the transaction bounce 3 days later, if there is a delay in the actual processing of the transaction.

When Can You Begin Trading

Once your account has been credited by the FX dealer, you are ready to begin trading. This is done directly through the dealer's platform and often happens relatively quickly after you have initiated funding. You can trade 24 hours a day on business days. The beginning of the trading week starts in the late afternoon on Sunday US Eastern time, when the markets in New Zealand open. These are going to be quickly followed by the market in Sydney, Australia, and Singapore, and then a little bit later, you will have Tokyo, Japan, and Hong Kong opening. London will be opening around 2 AM Eastern US time. You will be able to trade until the markets in New York close on Fridays, ending the trading week. So you have six days a week, 24 hours a day on most days to trade. This means that its always active and you can trade at hours that are the most convenient for your purposes.

Some Well-Known FX dealers

In this section, we will take a look at a few of the well-known FX dealers that operate inside the United States. Some of them are also stock brokerages. I have to be honest that while there are many good options,

I tend to favor the stock brokerages because these are solid companies that have been around for a long time. Also, if you are also trading stocks or options, it can save you a little bit of hassle, since you can have one brokerage to handle everything that you are doing. That said, some people like to keep their Forex activities separate from other trading activities. The way you set this up is entirely personal, and so there are no rules to follow, other than selecting a well-respected and legitimate dealer.

Forex dealers are regulated in the United States. This is done by the National Futures Association, and also by the Commodity Futures Trading Commission. The regulation of these dealers helps to ensure that there are some protections in place for individual traders. Not to pick on the Bahamas, and I am sure there are many legitimate companies operating in the Bahamas, but when you put your money in an overseas outfit that is not as tightly regulated, you put yourself at risk for being swindled, loss of capital, and lack of the kinds of protections that you get in the United States. There is definitely a balance between regulation and freedom, and you wouldn't want a situation where there is little to no regulation, when it comes to the handling of finances. Or even where there is regulation, but it is not enforced. One of the good things about the major Forex countries is that there is a pretty good balance between regulation and freedom to trade, and there is also a lot of solid protection for the investor. This assures that trades run smoothly and that the broker is handling every trader's money fairly and reliably.

A Forex broker is required to register. If a foreign broker is operating in the United States, that is serving clients who are residents of the United States; they must also register with the Commodity Futures Trading

Commission. You can check to verify that such registration has taken place. If you find a website and cannot verify that it is registered, this is not a website you should use for your trading purposes.

You can check the status of any FX dealer on the Background Affiliation Status Information Center. The web address is here:

https://www.nfa.futures.org/basicnet/

We can start upfront by considering well-established brokers, and you probably know some of their names. Some are even publicly traded companies. These brokers are not only very well established and trustworthy, but they will offer you a full suite of advanced tools that will help you do analysis and charting. We will get into this later, but you are going to want a broker that gives you important information that you can use to evaluate the trading situation at any moment. This is going to include the ability to use technical indicators and candlestick charts, the essentials used by experienced Forex traders.

Let's look at our first trading platform. It is offered by TD Ameritrade. This company was formed way back in 1973. Initially, it was created for trading on the stock market, and millions of people are still using TD Ameritrade for that purpose. Since its founding, it has expanded into many different areas of interest. When you sign up for an established platform like TD Ameritrade, you can be assured of many things. The first is that the company is definitely legitimate and registered. Second, they are under regulatory scrutiny to ensure that they treat small investors fairly. Since they also have a stock market trading platform, they are regulated by the SEC as well. The SEC does not regulate Forex trading and won't be directly looking into the Forex activities of TD Ameritrade, but the point is the company is well known to regulators.

Regulation of their Forex activities will be done by the Commodity Futures Trading Commission and the NFC.

TD Ameritrade will provide all of the tools you need to be a successful trader. This is going to include full capacity charting tools, candlestick charts, and all the technical indicators you need. They also offer customer support and access to third-party platforms that can be used to do research. You are going to be needing to look into the news, economic events, and other issues when doing Forex trading, and while you shouldn't obsess on it, it's a good idea to be informed.

TD Ameritrade also runs a trading platform called think or swim that allows you to trade stocks, options, and Forex. This is a popular platform with many tools of analysis that you can use on a desktop computer or via mobile application.

Ally Invest is another established brokerage run by Ally Bank. In addition to be a well-respected bank and giving you a lot of powerful tools, Ally Invest includes a practice trading platform you can use to practice trading before investing real money. There is some controversy over the value of this, but I generally recommend starting with a practice account for a short time, so you can get familiar with the process.

One of the most popular dealers for trading is FOREX.com. You may have heard of a trading platform called metatrader 4. This is available as a desktop app and as a mobile application. It's one of the most popular ways to trade Forex. It is fully integrated with FOREX.com. This website is highly trusted and operated by GAIN Capital Holdings, which is a publicly-traded company.

There are many other reputable dealers. You will have to take some time to research this on your own, but if you are already trading stocks with a brokerage, the first step that you should probably consider is looking to see if the broker you are already using offers Forex/currency trading. If the answer is yes, then this is certainly an acceptable path forward.

Spreads

Later we will discuss spreads, but this is the way that brokerage dealers charge commissions on Forex. So when looking for a reputable dealer, you are also going to be wanting to take a look at the spreads they charge and compare them in between your options.

No matter what happens, as long as you have selected a good brokerage, this should not be too much of an issue.

Summary: What to Look for When Choosing a Dealer

This list can be called the necessary qualities list; it's not necessarily comprehensive.

- It should be an established dealer that is registered on the BASIC site.

- It should have a long history either directly dealing in currency trading or as an established stock brokerage/bank.

- They should have reasonable spreads (aka commissions).

- The platform should offer lots of tools for analysis, including charting tools and technical indicators.

- They should offer access to research tools, but if they aren't available, you can read financial news and find information about currencies on many financial websites.

- While not required, if they have a demo or practice trading account, that is definitely a plus to consider.

- If they have a social platform or forum where you can post and ask questions, and see what other traders are thinking, that can be helpful as well.

What's Next

In the next chapter, we are going to introduce the basics of currency trading. So we will learn how to read currency quotes, the units used, and how trading is carried out in different sizes.

Chapter 3: Currency Pairs and PIPS

In the first chapter, we learned about the fact that on Forex, trading occurs in pairs. In the business, these are called currency pairs. Prices are always in terms of the price of one currency relative to another. Learning how to read and understand quoted data is important, and you need to have a thorough understanding of what everything is referring to. The good thing is that this is not really very complicated, so most readers will pick it up in a short amount of time. In addition to learning about currency pairs, we will need to learn how prices are quotes and the all-important "pips" that you may have heard about when people discuss Forex. We will get started by looking at currency pairs first.

Currency Pair Trading

When you are trading currency, you are trading one currency against another. So what does this mean? Essentially, you buy one currency and sell the other simultaneously.

You need to understand how you would buy or sell currency pairs based on the market conditions that you are anticipating. Let's use the Euro and US Dollar currency pair as an example.

If you believe that the Euro will strengthen against the US Dollar, then you would buy the EUR/USD currency pair, which means you are buying Euros and selling dollars. Conversely, if you believe that the Dollar is going to strengthen against the Euro, or put another way that the Euro will weaken against the dollar, then you would sell the EUR/USD currency pair. In that case, it means that you are selling Euros and buying dollars.

Currencies are priced relative to one another, and they are always quoted in pairs. For example, the Euro and the US Dollar are one of the currency pairs. Currency pairs are ordered, and the ordering is always the same. For the Euro and the US Dollar, it will appear like this:

EUR/USD

The currency on the left side is the primary, or base currency. The currency on the right side is the secondary. The order never changes, this is just the standard, and it's for trading and ordering purposes only. So you will not see USD/EUR quoted. It does not have anything to do with one currency value versus another or anything of the sort. The ordering of the pairs has the practical significance that we described above. So if you want to buy Euros because you think that the Euro is going to go up with respect to the dollar, then you buy EUR/USD. Or consider the pair GBP/AUD, which pairs the Great British Pound and the Australian Dollar. If you think that the Great British pound is going to go up against the Australian Dollar, then you would buy the currency pair. That means you are buying Great British Pounds and selling Australian Dollars. On the other hand, if you believe that the Great British Pound is going to go down with respect to the Australian Dollar, then you would sell the currency pair, meaning that you're selling Great British Pounds and buying Australian dollars.

The US Dollar is currently considered the worlds "reserve" currency, and as such, it is involved in some 88% of all currency trades every single day. The Euro and Japanese Yen are also involved in a lot of trades, but they come in at 31% and 22% of trades, respectively. The top ten currencies that are traded, based on the fraction of trading include the US Dollar, the Euro, Japanese Yen, Great British Pound (or Pound sterling), the Australian dollar, the Canadian dollar, the Swiss Franc, the Renminbi (China), and the New Zealand dollar. The fraction of trading that each of these currencies represents drops off very quickly as we move down the list. For example, the Canadian dollar only makes up about 5% of daily trades. Of course, you also have to remember that the daily volume on the Forex markets is $5 trillion, and so 5% of that still represents a large sum of money - $250 billion every day. So there is money to be made on a lot of currencies, you don't just have to focus on pairs involving the USD and Euro.

Many of these currencies are referred to by nicknames that are of historical origin. It's good to know what these nicknames are in case you get involved with conversations about currency trading, as experienced traders may throw around this terminology. You would not want to be lost in a conversation because you didn't know what the nicknames are. You may also on occasion see the nicknames used in articles and such.

Some of the nicknames are obvious. The Australian dollar is often referred to in shorthand form as the Aussie. The US Dollar is known as the greenback. This name will not surprise anyone. The New Zealand dollar sometimes goes by the name Kiwi.

A couple of more obscure names exist as well. The Great British Pound, while sometimes known by the name pound sterling, also gets referred to by some as the cable. The origin of its term is moderately interesting. In the days when electronic communications networks were first being established, the name cable came about because trading was done by undersea cables between the U.S. and Great Britain, and so American bankers began referring to the Pound as the cable. Somehow this name has stuck through more than 100 years of usage.

Another interesting name is for the Canadian dollar, which sometimes gets referred to as the loonie. This comes from the name of the dollar coin that the country used to have with a duck on one side of the coin.

The Majors

The currencies of the main developed countries and the European Union are known as the "majors." These include the US Dollar, the Euro, the Japanese Yen, the Swiss Franc, the Australian dollar, the New Zealand dollar, the Canadian dollar, and the Great British Pound. The symbols used for these are USD, EUR, JPY, CHF, AUD, NZD, CAD, and GBP, respectively.

But when someone says the "majors" they are really talking about the currency pairs that these are involved in. The major currency pairs include:

- EUR/USD
- USD/JPY
- GBP/USD

- USD/CAD

- USD/CHF

- AUD/USD

- NZD/USD

The majors make up the vast majority of the trading on the Forex markets. But as you might imagine, there are many different currency pairs. In fact, they can number 100 currency pairs. There can be money to made trading currencies that are not majors. You have to be careful when looking at other currency pairs because you might find yourself in a liquidity trap.

You know from finance that liquidity is a measure of how quickly you can convert an asset into cash. Something that is readily converted into cash is highly liquid. Therefore, a gold bar is pretty liquid, you can run down to a precious metals store and sell it for cash right away. A house is less liquid. While it can be converted into cash, it might take some time to sell it. When the markets are hot, it might sell in a few days or weeks, but it could take months at other times. If you needed money to pay for a car repair, selling your house would not be a good strategy, but selling a gold bar would allow you to raise the money nearly immediately.

In the currency markets, liquidity means you can either buy back a currency pair (if you sold it to open your position) or you can sell it (if you bought it to open) quickly. As we will see, when you are watching currency pairs on the charts, the time frame over, which you may need to make a move to close your position, can be very small. So it's important to be able to move quickly.

Many people, including some experts that you might run into on the internet, might be promoting the idea that you can make money trading minor currencies, like the Mexican Peso. There is a lot of software out there that will find currency pairs that are trending for you. That is all well and good, except it's not so good if you are trying to enter a trade when you identify it forming, and it takes so long that by the time your order is filled, it's nearing the peak in a price increase. Alternatively, you might be following a trend, and it starts showing signs that the trend is coming to a reversal. That is the time to get out of the trade. But you might get in a situation where you can't close your position quickly because it's a currency pair with low liquidity.

For that reason, you might want to stay away from minor currencies. The action is in the majors, and one thing about the majors is you won't have to worry about the kinds of problems that I have just described. Liquidity also impacts the cost of trading. The less liquid a currency pair is, the higher the cost of trading it.

There are currency pairs that involve some of the currencies from developed countries, which do have relatively high trading volume. These are composed of the major currencies when they are paired with each other but not with the US dollar. These include:

- GBP/CHF: Great British Pound and Swiss Franc.
- GBP/CAD: Great British Pound and Canadian Dollar.
- GBP/AUD: Great British Pound and Australian Dollar.

- GBP/JPY: Great British Pound and Japanese Yen.

- EUR/GBP: Euro and Great British Pound.

- EUR/AUD: Euro and Australian Dollar

- EUR/NZD: Euro and New Zealand Dollar

- EUR/JPY: Euro and Japanese Yen

- EUR/CHF: Euro and Swiss Franc

- EUR/CAD: Euro and Canadian Dollar

- CHF/JPY: Swiss Franc, and Japanese Yen

- AUD/JPY: Australian Dollar and Japanese Yen

- NZD/JPY: New Zealand Dollar and Japanese Yen

- CAD/JPY: Canadian Dollar and Japanese Yen

Next, we come to the so-called "exotics." These are currency pairs between a major and a strong economy that isn't considered one of the majors. So the USD or Euro can be paired with each of these currencies. Some of the "exotics" include Sweden, Norway, Singapore, Hong Kong, Denmark, South Africa, and Turkey. The exotics are not traded as much and so can be considered to be illiquid. As a beginning trader, they are probably best avoided. Some currency pairs that you will see include the Mexican Peso (MXN) and the Chinese currency (sometimes called the Yuan) CNH.

It doesn't end there, of course; you can trade currencies for nearly every country on earth that has one, so, for example, you could trade the Mexican Peso in one of its currency pairs. However, these currency pairs may be illiquid as well. As long as you can get in and out of the trade quickly, it's considered to be a good currency pair.

Summary: How Currency Pairs Work

Let's set up a hypothetical or generic currency pair to review the basic concepts.

(currency one)/(currency two)

When you say you are buying the currency pair, that means you are buying currency one and selling currency two. You will do this if you believe that currency one will rise in value with respect to currency two.

Or put another way, you believe that currency two is going to drop in value, relative to currency one. The currency pair is always quoted in this manner.

If you believe that currency two is going to rise in value with respect to currency one, then you would sell the currency pair. This is a bet that currency one is going to decline in value relative to currency two.

If the currency pair in question was EUR/CAD, buying the pair means you are betting on the Euro, and selling the pair means you are betting on the CAD.

It might sound a little bit like we are beating a dead horse, but this concept is important. Let's think about how this is going to work out in a chart. The Forex market will let you look at charts of currency pairs, and they look a lot like stock market charts. But it's important to understand the direction of the curve since we are talking about pairs.

If we have a chart for A/B, then if the curve is going up, that indicates an increasing price for the currency pair A/B. And what that means is that currency A is increasing in value, while currency B is decreasing in value. If you had bought the currency pair A/B, then this would be a winning trade for you.

On the other hand, if the curve was going downward, this would be favorable for currency B – indicating that it was going up while currency A was going down in value.

Remember that everything is relative when it comes to currency trading, there are not absolutes. So it's all about the price of once currency relative to another. That may or may not impact other currency pairs.

Here is an example: the chart below is for the AUD/USD currency pair. On the left-hand side, the price is decreasing, by a lot, but on the right-hand side, it made a steep climb upwards. Using what we just learned, you realize that on the left side of the chart, the value of the Australian Dollar was decreasing relative to the US Dollar, or you could put it in terms of saying the US dollar is increasing relative to the Australian Dollar. So on the left-hand side of the chart, if you had bought the currency pair, you probably would not have been too happy at that point. But if you had sold the currency pair – and therefore favored the US Dollar, for that time frame your bet was favored.

Meanwhile on the right side of the chart, as the curve is moving upward, if you had bought the currency pair, you'd be happy because an upward trend of the pair means that it was increasing in value — the Australian dollar was rising against the US Dollar. If you had sold the pair, well, in this case, you were losing money.

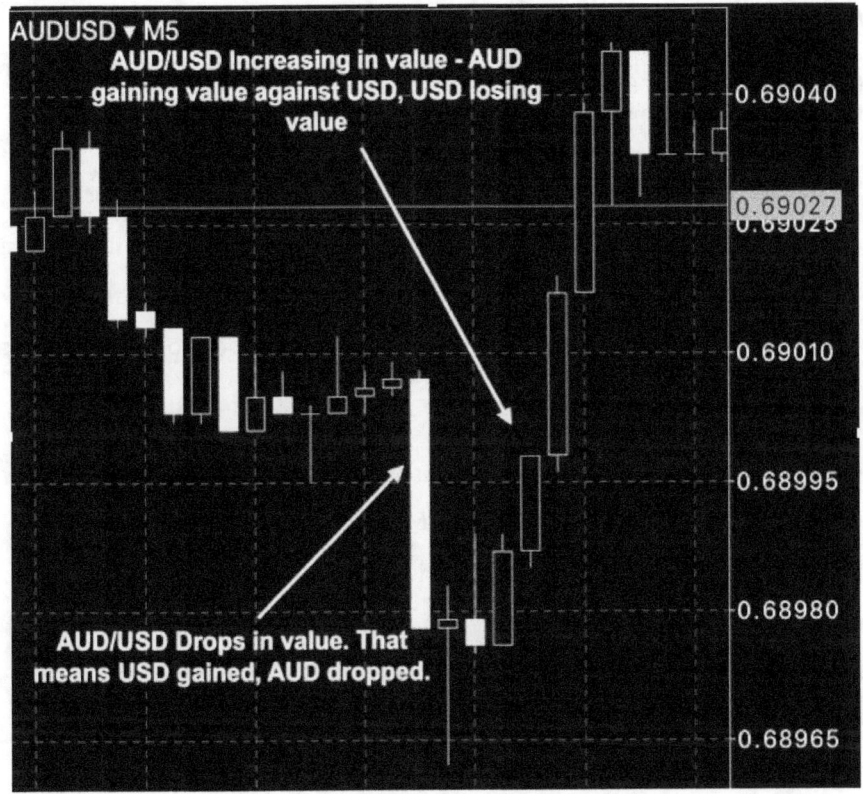

The price of the pair is listed on the right-hand side. This means one Australian dollar is worth $0.69 in US dollars. You can invert that (1/0.69) to express how many Australian dollars a US dollar would buy; the answer is 1.45.

PIPS

If you get into Forex trading, the concept of a pip is one of the most important that you will come across. Essentially, a pip is a measure of a price change in a currency pair, and it can be considered to be the most significant measure to make. Small pips mean big money when you are trading lots of currency. So it is crucial to understand a pip. We might begin by asking what does this phrase mean. It is nothing more than an acronym, and you must familiarize yourself with what it stands for.

PIP Means *percentage in point*. It can also mean the price interest point, but most people think of it in terms of percentage in point. In truth, most traders probably don't think about the formal definition, but they know how to work with pips and what the meaning is, when looking at prices of currency pairs.

To understand how to use pips on a practical level, you must look at how currency pair prices are quoted. Most currency pairs are actually quoted to five decimal places. It used to be four decimal places, but this has changed in recent years. One pip is a one-point change in the fourth decimal place. Let's suppose that the EUR/USD pair is quoted as:

1.14671

This is not real value; I have made this up for illustration purposes. The number to note is number 7, which lies in the fourth decimal place. This is the pip. If this value were to change to:

1.14681

Then there has a been a 1 pip move for the EUR/USD currency pair. We can practice some more. If the price moves to:

1.14781

It has changed in price by 0.00100. That is, the price went up by 10 pips. Now suppose that it changes to:

1.14731

If you take the difference, you get 0.00050 – that is, the price has dropped by five pips.

You are already becoming an expert at Forex trading. But you will notice that we have added a fifth number. The firth number is called the "pipette." Sometimes, the pipette is shown in a smaller font. Generally speaking, the pipette is not all that important. You can do well in Forex trading without worrying about pipettes. It is such a small number that it hardly matters for anything, but at least you know that it is there and what it is called. So if someone calls you and says that the GBP/JPY pair moved by 1 pipette, you know that the 5th decimal place has increased in value by one. But does it mean anything to the trader, as far as gaining or losing money? Not really.

Japanese Yen

When learning about pips, there is a special case of the Japanese Yen. In this case, pips are treated differently than they are for every other currency. The reason that this is so is quite simple. This has to do with the value or scale of the Japanese Yen as compared to other currencies. The Japanese Yen is a smaller currency than others that are traded. You might think of this by imagining that instead of the US Dollar, the 25-cent coin was the standard measure of US currency. That is all it is, and it's no more complicated than that; the Japanese Yen is just denominated at a smaller level.

It is quite a popular currency. So it pays to know where the pip is for the Japanese Yen, since it is quite a bit different from the pips of the other currencies. The special rule here is this. For the Japanese yen, the 2d decimal place is the pip. The third decimal place is the pipette. So if you see a quote for Japanese Yen that was, say:

110.873

The pip, in this case, is the number in the second decimal place, which would be 7. The pipette is the number that is found in the third decimal place. So in this example, it is 3. Now suppose that our price quote undergoes the following transformation:

110.893

This means that the price has risen by 2 pips. If it now goes to:

110.894

That means it has risen by one pipette. Now suppose there is a further change in the value. This time it goes to:

110.853

This time, it has dropped four pips, and also by one pipette. Do you see how simple this is? To be truthful, Forex trading is so simple that a child who has not yet entered high school can grasp the basic facts of Forex trading. Show this to your children, and they will learn all about pips and pipettes.

How Traders Talk About Pips

You are going to hear different conversations about pips when you are following the Forex markets. Included in this discussion is going to be some talk about how the price of a currency pair has changed. Right now, I am looking at the USD/RUR currency pair. RUR is the Russian Ruble. In this case, the value is:

63.54494

What is the pip? Try and figure it out before I give you the answer. This will test whether or not you are gaining knowledge. You can stop reading here if you need to.

Remember that for any currency pair other than the Japanese Yen, the pip is the fourth decimal place. Therefore, the pip is 9 in this case.

What if a trader told you that the US/RUR currency pair moved 50 pips? What on earth does this mean? It simply means that we add 50 pips to the value above. This is done by adding to the fourth decimal place, but it's the third since it's a power of ten.

Moved by 50 pips -> 63.54494 +0.00500 = 63.54994

Of course, I am saying that it went up by 50 pips. This might be a bit of assumption; it could have gone down 50 pips, the trader used the word "moved." Without further information, this could be the assumption to make. But you may ask to get clarification, if you are not completely sure of the direction of movement. If it went down 60 pips instead, then we would see a price movement in the following manner:

Down 60 pips -> 63.54494 - 0.00600 = 63.53894

And what is the pipette in this case? It is the number in the fifth decimal place, which is 4.

Price Quotes, Spread, Buying, and Selling

When you bring up price quotes for a currency pair, you are going to see them in two columns. Here is a real-time list of quotes from meta trader 5 that I have pulled up while writing this book:

EURUSD	1.11399	1.11404
GBPUSD	1.21823	1.21832
USDCHF	0.99137	0.99146
USDJPY	108.775	108.782
USDCNH	6.88852	6.88988
USDRUB	63.54402	63.55333
AUDUSD	0.69054	0.69061
NZDUSD	0.66299	0.66311
USDCAD	1.31665	1.31671
USDSEK	9.48899	9.49212
EURRUB	70.726	70.749
USDRUR	63.54494	63.55455
USDHKD	7.82281	7.82290

For a new trader, this can be a bit confusing. We will now explore what these numbers mean. If you are trading Forex, these are the types of price quotes that you are going to see on your trading platform. Therefore, it is important to know what they mean so that you are not in for any surprises when you trade a currency pair. Let us look at the top number, which is the famous EUR/USD currency pair, that makes up something like 35% of all currency trades on most days.

On the left-hand side, we see 1.11399. But on the right-hand side, we see 1.11404. What are these two numbers? It turns out that the number that is shown as the price on the left-hand side of a currency pair quote is the selling price. So in this example, 1.11399 is the selling price for the EUR/USD currency pair. The other price, which is found in the column on the right-hand side, is the buying price. The buying price is always going to be higher than the selling price!

This difference in price is called the spread. So to compute the spread, enter the value on the right-hand side into your spreadsheet or calculator. Then subtract the value on the left-hand side. That will tell you what the spread is for each currency pair.

For the Euro and US Dollar pair, we have the following spread:

$1.11404 - 1.11399 = 0.00500$

The 5 is in the third decimal place. The pip is the fourth decimal place. So it's a power of ten higher. That means the spread, in this case, is 50 pips. So, it costs 50 pips more to buy the EUR/USD pair than it does to sell it. If you were to sell the pair, you'd receive the price 1.11399, while if you were to buy the pair, you'd have to put up 1.11404. Now, does that sound fair? Well, the Forex dealer has to make their money in one way or another, and this is the method used for charging commissions.

Let us choose another example. These are the price quotes from the USD/HKD pair that you can see in the figure. The quoted value in the left-hand column is the selling price.

ON the left side, we have 7.82281 for the USD/HKD pair. That means if you want to sell the USD/HKD pair, this is the price you will sell it for. On the right side, we see 7.82290. The fourth decimal place is the pip, so there is a 1 pip spread between these prices.

So what is a spread exactly? Our past conversations on this should give a pretty clear hint. A spread is a markup price put there by the FX Dealer. I said it was a commission, but that is not really the case. When it comes to Forex trading, brokers actually make money from two things. They make money from the spread, that much is sure. But some brokers will offer tighter spreads. But brokers or Forex dealers, whatever you want to call them, are definitely not charities. They have to make money to stay in operation, and the fact is if they are giving you a smaller spread, they have to make up the money in some other way. This is done by charging a commission. This means that a Forex dealer or broker is going to make money from spreads and commissions.

Buying and Selling

The spread is something that is important to pay attention to. First lets us say what will happen if you enter a trade by various methods. Well, actually there are only two ways that you can enter the Forex trade.

The first method that can be used is buying the currency pair. If you buy the currency pair, then you are going to start the trade-up by a small amount, because the buy quote on the right-hand side is always a little bit higher than the sell quote on the left side.

So if the currency pair was the AUD/USD from the image above, the price quotes are listed here as:

0.69054 0.69061

We should immediately quote this in pips. There is a 1 pip difference here. The left side of this number pair, 0.69054, is the selling price. That is a bet that AUD/USD is going to drop in value. Or put another way, it's a bet that the Australian Dollar is going to drop with respect to the US Dollar. It can even be put in a third way still. That third way to say it is that you are betting that the US dollar is going to rise in value, as compared to the Australian dollar.

The left-hand number is the SELL price for the trade. So we could sell for 0.69054, which also means that we would be selling Australian dollars and simultaneously buying US Dollars.

The spread is important because if you sell to open a new position on the Forex market, that means we have to buy it back to close the trade. That is a little bit weird for new traders to wrap their heads around because most of us are used to the conventional way to use the stock market. That is, we buy stocks at a low price, and then we sell those stocks at a higher market price when the time is right.

But as we mentioned in the first chapter of the book, you can also short stocks. You can loosely think of a trade when you sell to open a currency pair as shorting the currency pair. We are hoping that it will drop in value because then when we buy it back, it will be cheaper and we make a profit on the difference. So this is very much like shorting the stock.

But if you will notice since the value quoted on the right-hand side, which is the buy price for the currency pair, is always higher than the price given for selling, that means you always open selling prices down by a given number of pips. That doesn't matter, typically the number of pips that you open down is going to be a small number. The values of these currency pairs can move by large amounts over the course of just one trading day. Just in the few minutes that I have been writing this passage, the prices quoted have changed. For the EUR/USD currency pair, you can remember that we started out with this:

1.11399 1.11404

Now it's already changed to this:

1.11415 1.11420

The selling price, which would be the price on the left-hand side here, has risen by 1 pip and 6 pipettes. On the other side, the buying side, its risen by 2 pips. The spread has, in fact, narrowed a bit.

If you buy a currency pair, obviously you have to sell it back in order to close a trade. So buying a currency pair is more along the lines of conventional thinking, that is it will be like the buy low, sell high mentality.

You have to wrap your mind around both modes of thinking, however. You are simply not going to want to be buying currency pairs all the time, because circumstances are always changing. So while one day it might be advantageous to buy a currency pair, a few days later it might be far better to sell a currency pair. Therefore, it will become important to understand the concept of selling to open a trade, and then buying it back to close the trade.

But in currency exchanges, it is really not all that mysterious. If you sell to open the USD/RUR currency pair, that means you are selling US Dollars to buy Russian Rubles. If you buy to open the currency pair, then you are buying US Dollars and selling Russian Rubles.

It really is that simple, and when you sell to open you star the trade down a bit.

Some brokers will offer a rebate. This means that some of the spread will be paid back to the trader. Please check with your individual broker for details.

SWAPS

Another concept that you have to become familiar with when it comes to Forex trading involves what are called swaps. A swap is involved with the payment of interest rates. When you hold currency, that means that you can earn interest on the currency. Well, to be honest, it depends on the situation. You need to know the interest rates in each country of the currency pair in order to determine whether or not you will earn interest. Consider the following currency pair, for the sake of our discussion here:

GBP/CAD

This currency pair is the Great British Pound and the Canadian Dollar. Now for the sake of argument, say that you have bought the currency pair. If you have a higher interest rate for Great Britain, as compared to Canada, that would mean that you would earn interest overnight. For the sake of example if the interest rate in Great Britain was 3%, but it was 2% in Canada, that means that if you old the currency pair overnight, you will earn 1% interest.

But you can pay interest on currency pairs held overnight as well. If the interest rates were switched, that is if the interest rate in Great Britain was 2% and the interest rate in Canada was 3% - and we bought the currency pair, then that would mean that if we held it overnight, we would have to pay interest.

If you sell the currency pair, then the opposite situation holds. If Great Britain has a higher interest rate than Canada, and you sell the currency pair GBP/CAD, and you keep your position overnight, then you would owe interest. On the other hand, if Great Britain had a lower interest rate than Canada, and you had sold the currency pair, then you would earn interest overnight.

This might sound like important talk, but the reality is that it's not going to be that important for most Forex traders. And that is probably going to include yourself. The reality is that the amounts of interest that we are talking about here tend to be very small. This is true generally speaking and to be quite honest about this; it's even truer now. The reason is that most central banks throughout the world are charging low-interest rates.

So the only time this is going to be important is if you are making large trades, and you hold the position for a long time period. If you hold the position for a long time, then each night that rolls over there will be a new calculation of interest either paid or received. So on one time, it might be small, but small things can add up. Therefore, if you hold your position for 120 days, then it will add up 120 times, and this could possibly make a difference. But even then, it's going to be a small amount of money, relatively speaking. I will say that in today's environment of small interest rates, and small differences in interest rates between the major central banks, that nobody is going to get rich trying to earn interest in this fashion.

Chapter 4: PIPS, Micros, Minis, and Standard Lots

Now we need to become familiar with the way that prices are calculated to buy amounts of currency. When you buy currency or sell it, this is done in "lots." Consequently, it becomes necessary to have an understanding of the different lot sizes that there are in Forex trading. There is also a number of pips that are associated with each lot size, and this will convert into a dollar amount. So you can imagine that you must understand this in order to be able to trade and know what you are doing.

Lot Sizes Used When Trading Currency

There are three trade sizes that are used in Forex trading. These can be micro, mini, and standard sizes. These are also referred to as lots. Each lot size represents a number of "units" of currency. There will be a price per pip that is given as well. These generally increase by a factor of ten in each case. So a mini is going to be ten times that of micro, and a standard lot will be ten times the size of a mini. The trade size can also be described as the volume of currency that you are buying or selling.

Price Per Pip

One of the relations that you need to know is the price per pip. This will be expressed as dollars or pips, or you can list the number of pips for $1.

Micro Lot

A micro lot is 1,000 units of currency. There are 10 pips for one dollar for a micro lot. That can be put another way, in saying that there is one pip for ten cents, so you have:

10 pips = $1

What this number actually means is that if you make 10 pips on a micro lot, you make one dollar. Of course, when trading, you can lose money as well, so if you lose 10 pips, that means you lose one dollar. These price quotes are only for micro-lots only.

The volume of a micro lot is 0.01. That is, it is 0.01 of a lot. This will make more sense when we look at the size of a standard lot.

Mini Lot

A mini lot is 10 times larger than a micro lot, therefore its 10,000 units of currency. Since a mini lot is ten times larger than a micro lot, that means that the volume of a mini lot is 0.10. Also, rather than 10 pips per dollar, for a mini lot, you have one pip per dollar. If you make 10 pips on a mini lot, then you make $10. Alternatively, if you lose 10 pips on a mini lot, that would mean you lose $10.

Standard Lot

The standard lot is the largest of the lot sizes. It is called standard because when Forex trading began, this was the only lot size that there was. The mini and micro lot sizes came later, in order to accommodate smaller traders. Once again, we increase everything by a factor of ten each time that we increase a lot of size. So since we know that a mini lot is 10,000 units of currency, and we also know that a standard lot size is ten times as big as a mini lot, that will tell you that a standard lot is going to be 100,000 units of currency.

The volume is also ten times larger. The volume of a mini lot was 0.1, and so the volume of a standard lot is 1.0. This makes perfect sense since, before the invention of the mini lot and the micro lot, the standard lot was simply a lot – so you have one unit of volume with a standard lot.

You can also look at this in the following way. A standard lot is simply a lot, and a mini lot is 10% of the volume of the standard lot, so the volume is 0.10 lots. Then the micro lot is 10% of the size of a mini lot, or 1/100 of the size of a standard lot, meaning that the volume is 0.01 lots.

Now you can see where the currency units come from. Start from the standard lot, which is 100,000 units of currency per lot. A mini lot is 10% the size, so you just multiply 0.10 by 100,000 units of currency, which will give 10,000 units per mini lot. Finally, a micro lot is just 1% of the size of a standard lot, and so 0.01 x 100,000 units of currency give you 1,000 units of currency for a micro lot.

For a standard lot, 1 pip is worth $10. If you make 10 pips, you make $100. If you make 50 pips, you will make $500. If you lost 10 pips instead, you would lose $100.

Number of Lots and Pip Moves

One of the things you will have to understand is how the number of lots traded relates to a given move in pips. All you have to remember is the dollars per pip in order to quickly do the calculation. The calculations are so simple you can do them in your head, or on the back of an envelope. But you need to understand the calculations first and practice with them.

Let's say that you make a trade of 3 lots. What kind of lots you may be asking. This is the first question that should always be asked since the number of dollars per pip varies by lot size.

For the following example, we suppose that there is a 20-pip move. We suppose for these examples that the number of pops moved is going to be a movement that occurs in your favor.

With 3 lots, we can figure the amount of money made in each case. Starting with a micro lot, remember that there are ten cents per pip. So for a single lot, a 20-pip move would mean that we made:

20 pips x $0.10/pip = $2.

Now you multiply this by the number of micro-lots in the trade. For this example, we are using 3 lots. So the total amount of money earned is:

3 x $2 = $6.

You can see that this is not that complicated. To increase our understanding, let's take a look at how this would work out if we instead considered a situation of trading mini lots. The key factor to remember for a mini lot is the following relationship:

1 pip = $1

So a 20 pip move for a mini lot means:

20 pips x $1/pip = $20

Naturally, the figure is ten times as large as that seen with the micro lot. For 3 lots that have been traded, this will mean that we have the following in total:

3 x $20 = $60.

Once again, it is ten times as large. So if you trade 3 micro-lots and make 20 pips, you make $6, but if you trade 3 mini lots and you make 20 pips, you've made $60.

Finally, let's try the example with the standard lot. To review here, in this case, we have the following relationship between a pip and a dollar:

1 pip = $10

Now, a 20 pip move means that we earn, on a per-lot basis:

20 pips x $10/pip = $200

Since we traded 3 lots in total, that means we have a total income of:

3 lots x $200/lot = $600.

So this is not that complicated. If you make $1 from a trade of a micro lot, you will make $10 for a trade of a mini lot, and then you would make $100 on the same trade for a standard lot.

Account Sizes

You can have different account sizes based on the concept of micro, mini, and standard lots. A micro account is going to be an account that has $1,000 or less. A mini account is sized at about $5,000 to $10,000. A standard account is $20,000 and up.

For a beginner, it is usually advised by experts that you start with a micro account.

How Will Different Pip Moves Impact Your Account

When you have an account of a different size, then you need to know how different pip moves are going to impact the account. If your account gets overwhelmed, you can actually have the account shut down by the dealer. Substantial moves can happen all the time. It can be a simple news item that sets things off. So you can have the federal reserve make an announcement, and this could cause a 100-pip move. So you need to be able to calculate what a 100-pip move will do to your positions, based on what lot sizes you are trading and the number of lots that have been traded.

Understanding Pips and Charts

Now let's take a look at a chart to look for pips. You need to be able to look at a chart and from there determine how many pips have moved in one direction or another, and then from there, you will need to be able to calculate how this move will impact your position in a given trade. For this example, let's have a look at the chart for the EUR/USD currency pair.

The chart shows some candlesticks which we will discuss later. For now don't worry about what they mean, you can just use your common sense in noting that the price is moving up and down the chart, and this is the price of the EUR/USD currency pair, so an upward move is favorable if you buy the EUR/USD pair, and a downward move is unfavorable. But if you sold the pair, you want the price shown on the chart to go down.

The price is shown on the right side of the chart. We have noted the pip position – the 4th decimal place – with the small white arrows. The opening price for this chart is on the far-left side, and it was 1.11400. So the pip is 0 at the open on the chart.

In the middle of the chart, it went up high and actually passed through the price we have noted with the dashed line, to 1.11440. So there is 4 pip move on the chart (it later drops down to 1.11417).

How would this 4-pip move translate if we bought 7 lots?

Let us begin with the micro-lots, and then we will consider mini lots, and then later we will consider standard lots. Beginning with the micro-lots, we start with the fundamental relationship in cost per pip, or if you want to say it as pips per dollar. For a micro lot, there are 10 pips per dollar, or as we said earlier, there is $0.10 per pip.

So a 4-pip move translates into:

4 pips x $0.10 per pip = $0.40

Since we are talking about trading 7 lots, this means that the total move on our trade is:

7 lots x $0.40 = $2.80

Now let's understand how this will work for a mini lot. Of course, you can always just multiply this by ten, and so you can jot down the answer now. But we should work through it using first principles in order to understand how to always do the calculation.

In this case, we want to start with the fundamental relationship that is given for mini-lots. That relation is that there is $1 per pip. Therefore, a 4-pip move translates into:

4 pips x $1/pip = $4

Now we multiply by 7 lots since that is the size of our trade, and the 4 pip move means that we have gained:

7 lots x $4/lot = $28

Finally, to do the same calculation for a standard lot, we begin with the relationship between pips and dollars. For the standard lot, there are $10 per pip. Therefore, we have:

4 pips x $10/pip = $40

For seven lots in our trade, we get:

7 lots x $40/lot = $280

So if you are trading micro-lots, a 4-pip move would mean a gain of $2.80 for a seven-lot trade. If you are trading mini lots is $28, and if you are trading standard lots, this would be a $280 move.

What if there was a 400-pip move? If you look online, you will see that there can be moves of this size over very short time periods. Let's say that it dropped 400 pips in a minute. How much money would you lose in a single minute for a 7-lot trade?

For a micro lot, we have:

400 pips x $0.10/pip = $40

With seven lots, the total loss would be:

7 lots x $40/lot = $280

Now let's consider the case of mini lots. Now we have the following:

400 pips x $1/pip = $400

With seven lots, the total loss would be:

7 lots x $400/lot = $2,800

You see that our losses are adding up quite substantially. Now let's go to a standard lot which has $10 per pip. In this case, we've got:

400 pips x $10/pip = $4,000

For a total of seven lots, the total loss is:

7 lots x $4,000 = $28,000

This example serves to illustrate the danger that Forex traders face, because yes, indeed, you can face a loss of 400 pips over a minute, and even over a few seconds. Such a loss could potentially wipe out your account.

This serves as an important example. The reason that it's important is too many novice traders are focusing only on the wins. And too many Forex gurus are more than eager to feed this mentality, by telling people what they want to here. Yes, there are two sides to every trade. And you could have been on the other side of this trade, which means that the 400-pip move would have worked in your favor to earn you a huge amount of money over a very short time period.

But the potential for catastrophic loss ought to give you some pause – you need to make sure that you are making trades that you can handle, and you should stay on top of your trades. Having too much riding on a single trade is going to be creating a situation that could cause very large problems down the road.

Currency Units Explained

We have defined how many currency units there are for a given lot size. Let's review these concepts. Starting with a micro lot, there are 1,000 currency units. A mini lot is ten times as large, and so a mini lot is 10,000 currency units. Finally, the standard lot is 100,000 currency units. Some readers who are brand new to the concept of Forex may be wondering what currency units are.

Quite simply, they are what the name implies. If you are trading US dollars, 1,000 currency units mean that you are controlling $1,000. So for a standard lot, that means if you are trading one lot, you are controlling $100,000. If you were trading five standard lots, that would mean that you would be controlling $500,000.

That is a pretty crazy concept, but as a beginning trader, you are going to start off with a micro account.

How to Start Your Trading

Beginners should start with a micro account and only make small trades. There is going to be a temptation there to use leverage to magnify your potential, but you should start off small and slowly. A beginner should be entering trades looking to make small gains and learning how to trade, not trying to have huge wins straight from the beginning.

Position Sizes

One of the important things to think about is the liberal use of leverage that goes on with Forex trading. Remember, in the stock market, the amount of leverage that is available is relatively small. On the stock market, you only have 2:1 leverage.

The size of a trade you can enter depends on the amount of your own cash that you put up. The cash that you put up to enter a trade is called margin. So if you put up $1,000 on an account with 2:1 leverage, you can take a $2,000 position. If the stock is $100 a share, with your own cash, you could have purchased 10 shares. But using leverage, you can borrow another $1,000 for a total of 20 shares.

As we mentioned in the introductory chapter, the amount of leverage that is available to Forex traders is much larger than that which is available on the stock markets. In the United States, it's 50:1. So if you put up $1,000 of your own money, that means you can take a $50,000 position.

Or if you are a small trader, if you put up $100 for a trade, then you can enter a position that is sized as:

$100 x 50 = $5,000

Brokers will have a minimum amount of cash that must be kept in the account. This is often referred to as the maintenance margin. When the value of the positions you hold and the cash you have falls below the maintenance margin, the broker will issue a margin call. A margin call is a requirement that you add more money to the account to bring it up to the maintenance level. Alternatively, you might be forced to sell some of your positions.

One problem with a margin call is that the broker can force you to exit a position even if you don't want to, in order to cover some or all of the deficit. So if a margin call happens, you won't be able to wait around for a reversal of a trade that isn't going your way. For this reason, if you are using leverage, you need to pay close attention to the way that things are going in your account.

How to Figure the Amount of Cash You Need to Enter a Trade

The first step is to determine the lot size and the number of lots that you want to do for the trade. Let's look at a few specific examples.

The key thing you need to do here is to look at the number of currency units, which is just dollars, if you are trading in the United States. So for a micro lot, its $1,000 per lot. If it's a mini lot its $10,000 per lot, and for a standard lot, it's $100,000.

Now let's say that you want to trade 5 micro-lots. You will also need the amount of leverage available, which is 50 in the United States. The first thing that you do is simply calculate the total amount of currency in the position. So this will be the number of lots multiplied by the amount of currency per lot. For 5 micro-lots we would have the following result:

5 micro lots x $1,000 per lot = $5,000

Now, you divide this by the leverage. Using 50, we would get:

$5,000/50 = $100

Therefore, to take a $5,000 position, you only need $100 in actual cash. Of course, the danger is when the trade works completely against you with a large move.

Let's do two more examples. In order to thoroughly illustrate the way this works, we will give an example of a trade of mini lots and a trade of standard lots. For a mini lot example, let's suppose that we want to trade 7 lots. Remember that for a mini lot there are 10,000 currency units per lot, so that is $10,000 and the total size of the trade would be given by:

7 lots x $10,000/lot = $70,000

That is a pretty sizable trade for a beginner. But how much actual cash do you need? There is no mystery here; we once again divide by the amount of leverage that is granted. In the United States, the leverage is 50:1, and so we divide by 50 to get the amount of cash that we need to deposit in our account:

$70,000/50 = $1,400

If you live in Australia or the UK, the leverage at the time of writing is 100:1, although there are discussions that indicate they may adopt the

50:1 standard used in the United States. But with 100:1 leverage, the amount of cash you would need is:

$70,000/100 = $700

This is an extraordinary result, even with just 50:1 leverage. This is one of the reasons that the Forex markets have such wide appeal to traders. You simply cannot get into a situation like this with the stock market. Consider Apple. It's trading at $209 a share. If you had $1,400 in your account, then you could buy:

$1,400/$209 = 6 shares

If you had 50:1 leverage (which you don't on the stock market, but we are imagining), then you could buy:

$70,000/$209 = 334 shares

That would be a remarkable result – if the stock went up to $10 a share over a given time period, you could make $3,349, as opposed to just $60 with no leverage. Sadly, the real leverage available on the stock market is only 2:1, and so you could only buy 12 shares using a margin account.

This difference in leverage is the power of Forex trading. So how much cash do you need to trade a single lot? This is easy to figure out. And the amount of cash that you need is not all that large, which is one factor that has opened up Forex trading to the masses.

First, for a micro lot, you can trade one lot if you put up:

$1,000/50 = $20

For a mini lot, you can trade one lot if you put up:

$10,000/50 = $200

And finally, for a standard lot, you can trade one lot if you put up:

$100,000/50 = $2,000

Notice that the power of tens always applies in Forex trading, when considering the different lot sizes. But this shows that we don't need much cash on hand to control large amounts of currency in a single trade. Now that I have spelled out the cash requirements for one lot of different sizes, you can just multiply the value given by the number of lots you want to trade. So if you want to trade 15 mini lots, then you need:

15 x $200 = $3,000

Understanding Trade Size Using Volume

Another exercise to do in order to get to know your way around the Forex markets is to use trade size to determine the amount of currency relative to the standard lot. This might seem a little pointless and boring, but it's important to be able to do these simple calculations so that you know your way around the markets. Let's use a mini lot as an example.

Remember that a mini lot has a volume of 0.1. So let's figure out the amount of currency that will be controlled, along with the amount of money you have to deposit in order to enter a trade that will involve 5 lots.

First, we multiply the volume by the number of lots:

0.1 x 5 lots = 0.5

Now we use the fact that a standard lot will be 100,000 currency units. The trading volume used to define micro, and mini lots are nothing more than the fraction of a standard lot. Therefore, five mini lots are:

Trading volume x standard lot currency units = 0.5 x $100,000 = $50,000

Then to determine the amount of money, actual cash, that we need to deposit in order to enter the trade, we divide by 50 when we are in a country that is using 50:1 leverage:

$50,000/50 = $1,000

To get familiar with all these numbers, just set up different trading scenarios to practice. The more you practice, the more automatic it will become. You want to make sure that you are accurate when figuring this out, in order to accurately determine what you are getting into when entering into a trade, and so that you actually know how large of a position you can actually enter into.

Your Account and Margin

You will see that Forex accounts display balance and equity, along with usable or free margin. The balance is the amount in the account before you have entered into any trades. Equity is the balance summed up with the value of open trades. This can be plus or minus, since a trade may be in the red. Finally, Usable or free margin is the amount of cash that you actually have leftover to make more trades. If you have a losing trade, the broker will use any free margin that you have to cover the losses.

Chapter 5: Understanding Charts

Before we begin an in-depth discussion of the strategies used by Forex traders, you need to have an understanding of charts. The charts used in Forex are similar in a superficial sense to the charts that you may have seen on the stock markets. Typically, Forex traders are going to be using candlestick charts. In fact, this is almost a universal practice. So the first thing that a beginning Forex trader needs to learn, beyond the basic fundamentals that we covered in the last two chapters, is how to read and understand Forex charts. That is the topic that we are going to cover in this chapter.

Remember What the Chart Is Charting

This sounds like a crazy statement, but you have to remember that the currency pair A/B means that if the value shown in the chart increases, this favors the currency A. What this means is that the value of currency A is increasing relative to the value of currency B. You can also look at it in the sense that if the graph on the chart is increasing, the value of currency B is decreasing.

So if you buy the currency pair A/B, and the increasing graph or upward trend is a trend that is working in your favor.

Now consider a downward trend. When the trend is going downward, you are losing money if you had bought the currency pair A/B, because this means that the value of currency A is decreasing relative to currency B.

Where some new traders get confused is when you sell the currency pair A/B. In this case, the meanings on the chart are reversed, because if you sell the currency pair A/B, this means that you are betting on the currency B. So when the chart is un an upward trend, if you had sold the currency pair you are losing money. This is easy to understand. For the sake of simplicity, let's say that you had sold the currency pair for $1. To exit the position, you have to buy back the currency pair. But if it increases in price to $2, then you would lose $1 buying it back. The values given here are for illustration only, but it nicely illustrates the general concept.

Now consider the opposite situation. That is, we are still talking about selling the currency pair A/B, but this time we see a downward trend on the chart. This means that the price of the currency pair is decreasing. We can, of course, frame this result in many ways. One of the ways that we can do so is to say that the currency B is increasing in value, with respect to currency A. Now let's say that once again we sold the currency pair A/B for $1. Now we imagine that is has decreased in price to $0.50. Then we can buy it back, and we make a $0.50 profit.

Of course, these prices are not realistic for a Forex trade, but it clearly shows the concept of how this actually works. If you understand the concept explained here, and you've understood how to read the change in pips from the chart and how to convert that into dollars moved based on your position size, then you are well on your way to becoming a Forex trader who at least understands what is going on.

What Is a candlestick

The next thing to come across is the use of candlesticks, which you always see on Forex charts. A candlestick is a graphical way to represent price action. By price action, we simply mean how high did the price go, how low did it drop, and what the opening and closing prices were. The candlestick charts also give a visual representation that we can eyeball, in order to see at a glance whether the price went up or down for a given time period.

So what each candlestick represents is a "trading session." The trading session can be one of many different lengths of time. Different traders are going to choose different lengths of time used for the trading sessions shown on the chart, depending on what their needs are. Some traders are interested in very short time frames, so they may use one-minute trading sessions. Others are going to use 5- or 15-minute trading sessions. You can also use 4-hour trading sessions or even one-day trading sessions. It's up to you to decide what time interval to use, and this is going to be decided in part by your trading style.

Before we show the basics of a candlestick, you need to understand how and why these are used. The basic idea that is behind the candlestick is to have a visual way to look at the chart and determine whether or not there is going to be a price reversal. Price reversals and trends are the bread and butter of this business. The first thing you are going to want to look for when you are trading currencies is if there is a trend one way or the other.

If there is a strong upward trend and there are signals that the trend is going to continue, then this is a currency pair that you want to buy.

Conversely, if there is a downward trend, this could be a currency pair that you want to sell. This little fact that we have described is one important way that Forex trading differs from stock market trading, at least for most people. Granted, there are many people who trade options or who short stock, and they will make more complicated market plays. But you see with Forex that it automatically offers you ways to make money, no matter which way the market is moving. It's always in pairs, and you don't have to be wedded to one single currency.

That means that you don't have to be focused only on the dollar and hoping that it's going to always rise with respect to the Euro. As a Forex trader, you really should not care which direction the currency is moving. You can earn profits either way. The only time you care about which direction it's moving is after you've entered a position. Then and only then is the time that you need to be concerned about this issue.

Trend reversals are really the important thing to look for. If the market has been in a downward trend for some time, and you have been sitting on the sidelines, you are going to be looking for a trend reversal. It's never a good idea to get involved in a trade when it's too late. If you have been following the currency pair A/B and the currency pair has been in a long time downtrend, even if you like the currency B, you are probably better off waiting for a reversal, and buying the currency pair, rather than joining the trend late in the game. So in this example, when the candlesticks gave you the signal that the trend was reversing, you would buy the currency pair. The trend reversal signal would indicate that the downward trend has come to an end, and now is the time to get in a position in order to take advantage of the coming upward trend.

Structure of a Candlestick

The candlestick has three parts. The first part is the rectangular area that is found in the center of the candlestick. This is called the body. The body of the candlestick tells you the opening and closing prices of the trading session. However, there are two types of candlesticks. Traditionally they are black and white, but I am going to skip over that because who uses black and white charts anymore. I can assure you that almost nobody does.

The background of most charts these days is either black or white. We are going to take the latter possibility, first because most Forex traders actually use black background charts. But you can use white backgrounds and some traders too.

There are two types of candlesticks. A candlestick can indicate that the price dropped for the trading period, in which case it is called a "bearish" candlestick. Or the candlestick can indicate that the price increased over the trading period, in which case it's a bullish candlestick.

On a chart with a white background, a bearish candlestick is red in color. A bullish candlestick will be green in color. On a black chart, the bearish candlesticks are usually solid white, and the bullish candlesticks are the green outline.

That is all pretty basic to understand. Now let us use a basic fact to explain the price action described or illustrated by a candlestick. If there is a bearish trading session, that means that the opening price was higher than the closing price. As a result, the top of the candlestick body — which is a higher pricing point — represents the opening price for the trading session. In contrast, the bottom of the candlestick, which is the lower price on the chart, represents the closing price for the trading session.

A bullish candlestick works in the opposite way. A bullish candlestick indicates that the price went up during the trading session. So the top of the candlestick is the closing price for the trading session. The bottom of the candlestick is going to be the opening price for the trading session.

A candlestick has lines that come out of the top and bottom of the body. These lines are called shadows or wicks. They have the same meaning whether or not the candlestick is bullish, or whether it's bearish. The wick or shadow coming out of the top of the candlestick body tells you the high price of the trading session. The bottom wick tells you the low price of the trading session. The basics of candlestick setup are shown below.

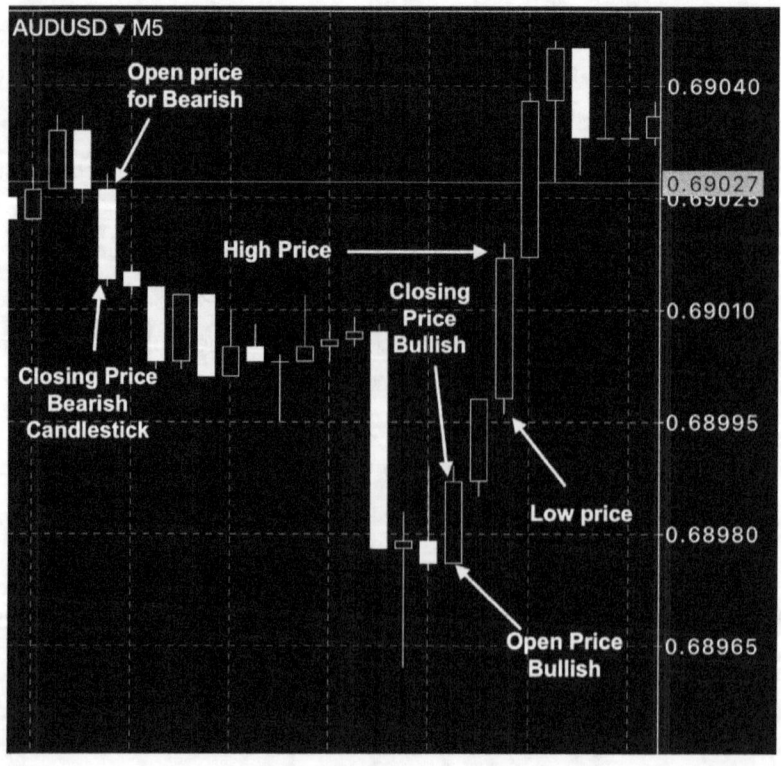

Reversal Signals

Now we need to be able to look for certain signals that indicate a coming change in price trend. The signals are in the price action that tells us that traders are adopting a different sentiment, and the price is about to change direction. This is something you can spend a great deal of time educating yourself about. However, there is only a small subset of indicators that you need to be aware of.

Bullish Reversal Signals

A bullish reversal signal occurs at the bottom of a downtrend, and it indicates that the trend is going to reverse, and prices will start rising. The first bullish reversal signal is called an engulfing candle. In this case, we don't pay any attention to the size of the wicks, but the size or length of the body is important. This is a two-candle pattern, with a bullish or green candle following a bearish or white/red candle. The size of the bullish candle should be such that the opening price is actually lower than the preceding closing price, so that at open of the trading session prices dropped. Then, the closing price should be higher than the opening price of the previous trading session. This indicates that there was a large amount of buying pressure that was pushing prices up.

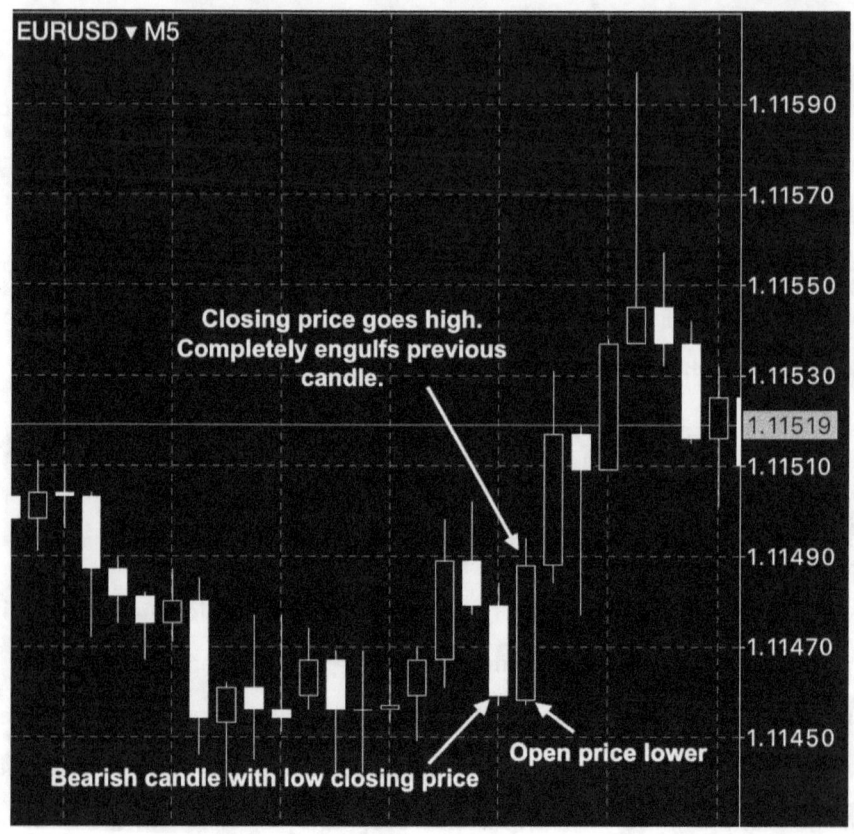

The second bullish pattern that we will consider is called a hammer. This is something to look at during a downtrend that may indicate that a reversal into an uptrend is about to start. A hammer has a short body, with a long wick to the bottom. This is significant because the long lower wick indicates that during the trading session, prices were pushed far downward. However, the session managed to close with a higher price than it opened with, because buying pressure overcame the strong selling pressure, and pushed prices higher.

An inverted hammer is another bullish signal, but it has a narrow body with a long top wick. In this case, there was strong buying pressure during the trading session, but it was pushed back down by selling pressure. However, the selling pressure was not strong enough to overcome the session, and it ends up closing with a higher price than it opened with.

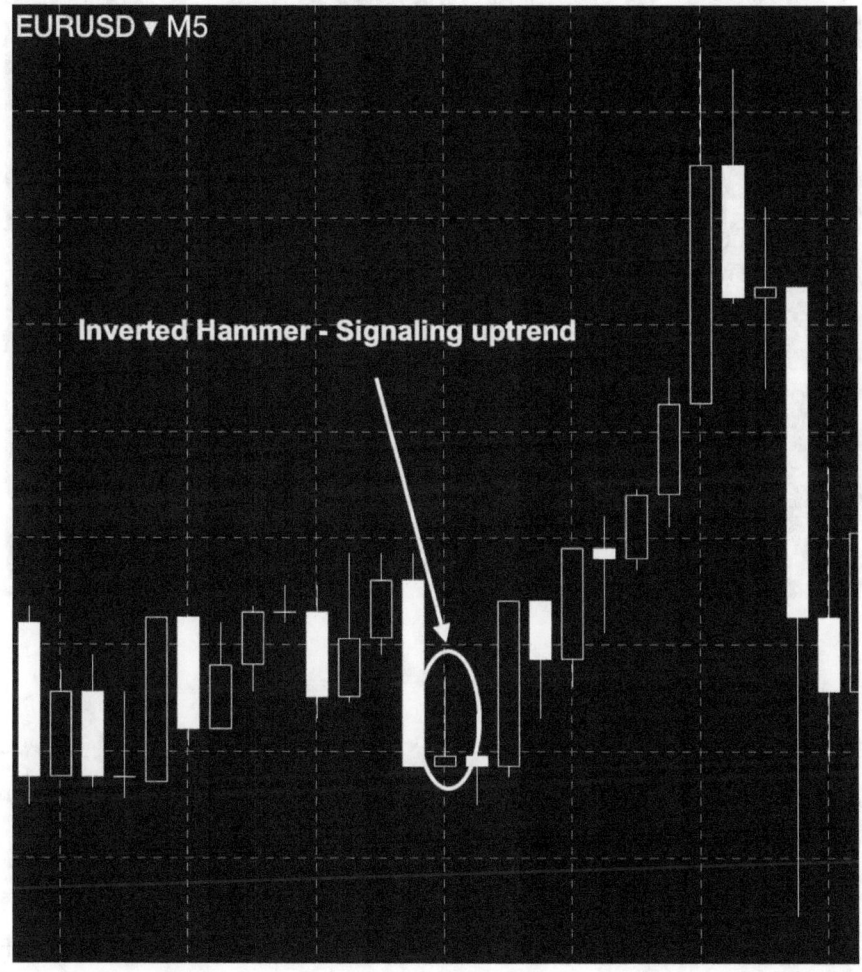

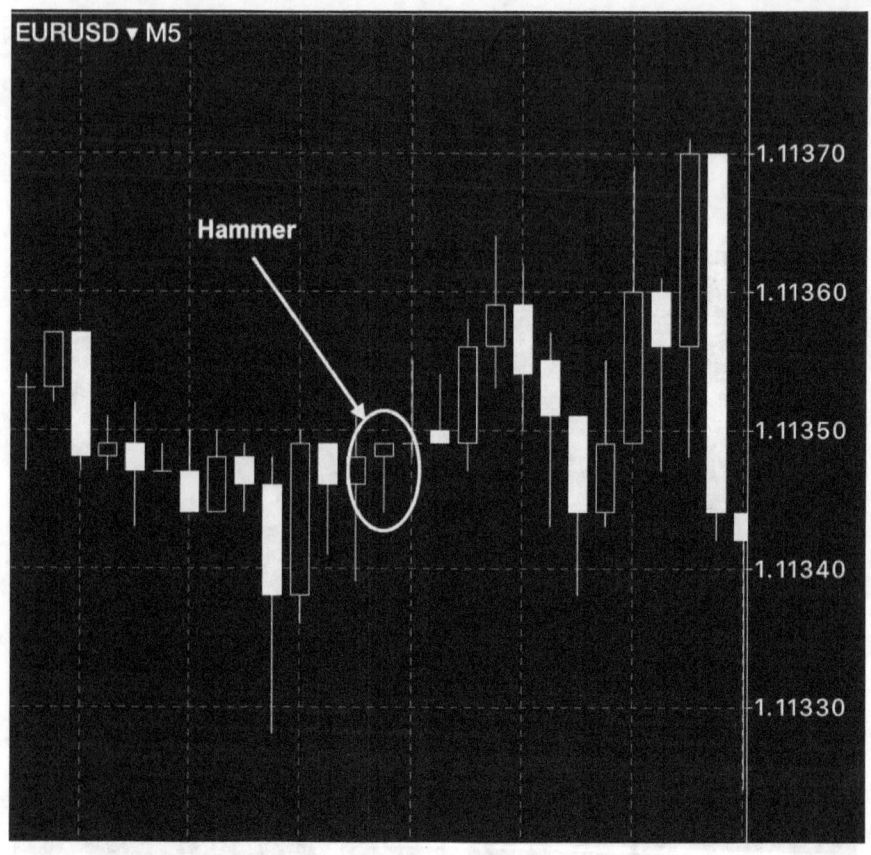

Another pattern to look for is called three white soldiers. The naming convention is unfortunate because bullish candles on Forex are green and bearish candles are white. However, in the old days of black and white charts, bullish candles were drawn as hollow boxes on white paper, and so were known as white candles. In those days the bearish candles were filled in with solid black, and so were known as black candles. Therefore, three white soldiers are going to be three successive bullish candles in a row, with successively higher prices. Nowadays on color charts, it will be three green soldiers.

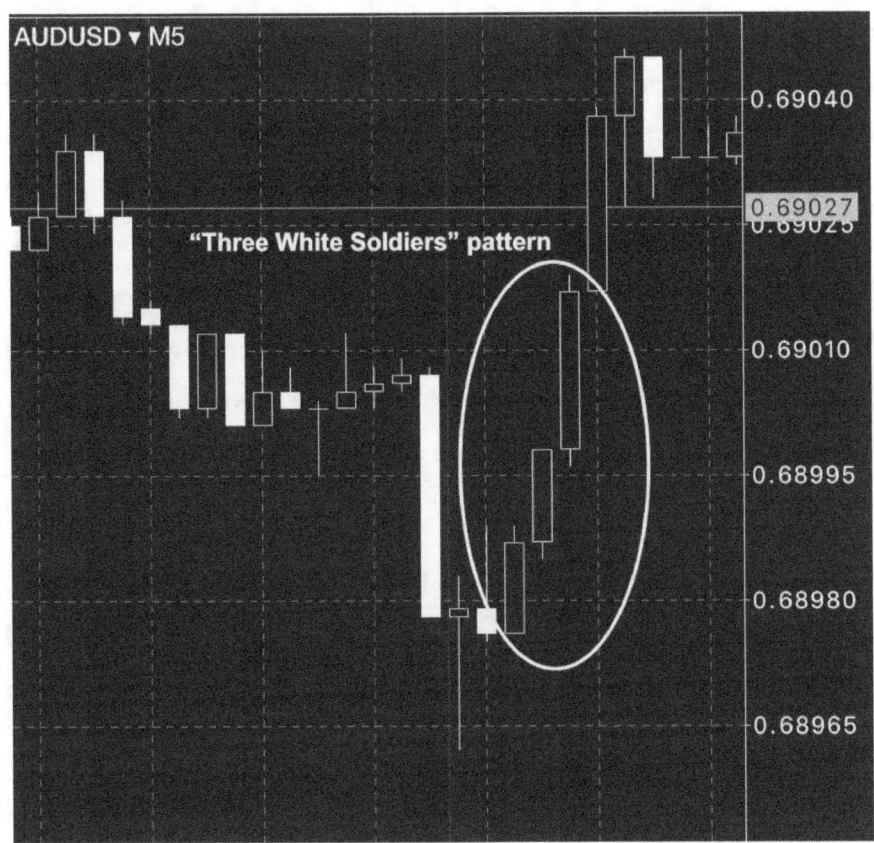

The next pattern to be aware of is called a piercing line. A piercing line is a bearish candle that is followed by a bullish candle, so on a black chart, it will be a white candle followed by a green candle. In this case, the bullish candle will open lower than the previous days close. But then, the price will be pushed high by buying pressure, and the session will close at a price that is at least halfway up the previous bearish candle or more.

The final bullish trend reversal signal that you need to be aware of is called a morning star. This is a pattern that involves a "doji," which is also known as an indecision candle. When you see a doji, there will be an opening and closing price that are very near to each other if not exactly the same. It may have long wicks on both sides, indicating that the price was pushed high by buying pressure, and it was also pushed low by selling pressure, but the closing price ended up at the same level as the opening price. This is why it is known as an indecision candle. Ideally, the high and low prices will be higher and lower than the opening price by the same amount. Sometimes you will see a single line with no wicks; this indicates that the open and closing prices were the same, and there was no pressure either way.

For a morning star pattern, you will have a bearish candle on the left. This will be followed by a doji, or indecision candle. This, in turn, should be followed by a bullish candle that opens at a higher price than the doji closing price, and then it closes higher.

Bearish Candlestick Patterns

Now we will describe bearish candlestick patterns. These are essentially going to be the same types of signals, but instead of looking for them at the bottom of a downtrend, you will be seeking them during an uptrend in prices. This will indicate that a downward trend in prices is coming. In each of the patterns, you would reverse the candlesticks, that is where you expect to see a green or bullish candlestick, in a bearish pattern you would look for white or red candlesticks.

One pattern you can look for is an engulfing pattern. In this case, we would be looking for a bearish candlestick following a bullish candlestick. Again, with an engulfing pattern, the size or length of the wicks is not important, you want to compare the body sizes of the two candles. In this case, the price should open higher than the closing price of the preceding bullish candle, but then the price should be driven low to a lower closing price that is lower than the previous opening price of the bullish candle.

The second pattern to look for is called a shooting star. In this case, you are looking for a bullish candle that forms an inverted hammer during an uptrend. This indicates that the session opened, prices were pushed up high, but then selling pressure pushed them low enough so that the trading session opened with a lower price than it opened with. You will note a shooting star by the long wick pointing upwards from a bearish candlestick with a relatively narrow body.

Three black crows are the analog to three white soldiers. Again, the terminology is unfortunate because almost everyone uses colored charts now, and bearish candlesticks are either white or red. In any case, what you are looking for now is a pattern with three bearish candlesticks in a row, with closing prices that are successively lower as you move forward in time. This indicates that as time is marching forward, there is increasing selling pressure, and this likely means that a downtrend is coming.

A hammer can also occur during an uptrend, in the form of a bearish candle. This is a classic hammer with a narrow body and a long downward wick. That shows that during the trading session, there was a large amount of selling pressure, pushing prices downward. Then prices reversed with buying pressure, but it was not strong enough to push prices back above the opening, so the session closed with a lower price than it opened with. This may indicate a coming trend reversal.

You can also look for the bearish piercing line, where a bearish candle follows a bullish candle. In this case, the opening price will be higher than the closing price of the preceding bullish candle, but then the closing price will end up at the halfway mark of the bullish candle or lower.

Candlestick Patterns – The Bottom Line

Candlestick patterns offer a wealth of information about trading trends, and if you intend to become a Forex trader, you should put the time in to thoroughly learn about candlestick patterns. However, keep in mind that they are as much art as they are science. Reading them accurately is going to be a skill that comes with experience.

The important thing to realize is that they are signals, but candlestick patterns are not rules. Most of the time, when you see a given candlestick pattern, this is going to indicate that there is a trend reversal coming, but many times you will see the pattern, and it won't happen. As a result, you should confirm candlestick patterns with other indicators, which we talk about in the next section.

Moving Averages

The main indicator tool that you want to include on your charts is called a moving average. A moving average takes the prices over a time period that you specify, and it computes the average at each point. So if you have a 7-period moving average at each point along the chart, it would take the previous seven prices, and average them to give value at the current point. The result of this type of calculation is that the normally jagged lines that you see on financial charts are turned into smooth curves that display the trend.

By comparing moving averages for different time periods, you can look for confirmation signals of a coming trend reversal. Typically, in Forex, people will use a 9-period and a 20-period moving average. The signals to look for are the movements of the short period average, with respect to the long period moving average. If the short period moving average crosses above the long period moving average, this is an indicator of a coming upward trend in price. On the other hand, if the short period moving average crosses below the long period moving average, then this indicates that there is a coming downward trend in price.

Some traders use what is termed a simple moving average. In this case, the prices are just averaged straightforwardly. However, the problem with this approach is that equal weight is given to prices, no matter how long ago they were in the past. Suppose that you were using a 200-period moving average with one-day trading sessions. If it were a simple moving average, that would mean that the price 200 days ago would have the same weight in computing the average as yesterday's price. This defies common sense, and as a result, most traders use other types of moving averages.

One of the most popular of the other types of moving averages is called an exponential moving average. This moving average tends to give more accurate information. The reason that it's able to do so is that the exponential moving average weights the prices. The mathematical details aren't important for traders to know, you only have to note that when you use an exponential moving average, prices that are closer to the current trading period are given higher weights than long ago prices. This means that an exponential moving average curve is going to emphasize recent prices, as opposed to long ago prices.

The use of moving averages is so common that trading platforms, like metatrader, are going to show them below your pricing chart by default. An example is shown below, with crossover points indicated by the white arrows.

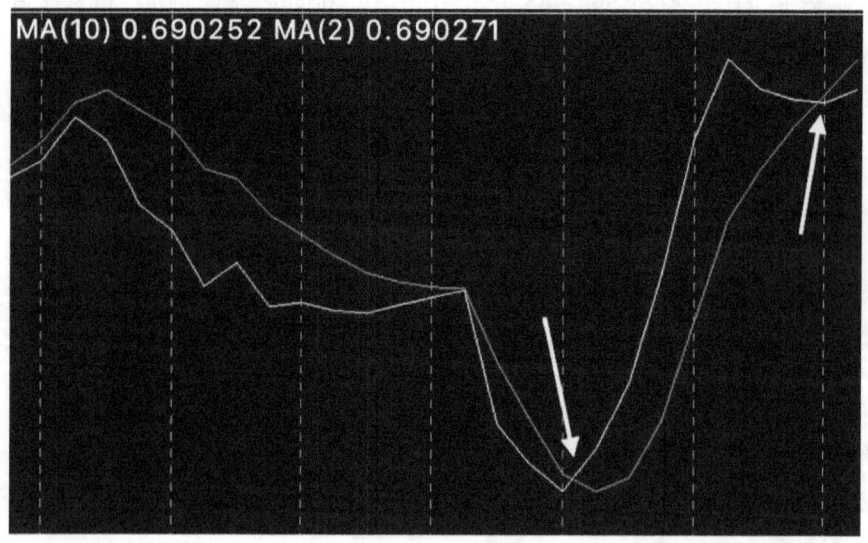

The way to do your analysis is to combine what you see with the candlesticks with what the moving averages are telling you. In my experience, the moving averages tend to be very accurate indicators of upcoming trends. However, it remains to be seen if the trend reversal is strong or long-lasting.

You can use a two-step process. The first step is to closely follow the candlestick patterns to look for indicators that a reversal is coming. If you see that the candlesticks are showing signs of a trend reversal, then you can check the moving averages to confirm or deny. If they confirm what you see on the candlestick charts, then you can make a move on a position, whether it is opening a new position or closing an existing position. As I said earlier, on most trading platforms, they are going to add the moving averages to your chart by default. So you can eyeball them with the candlesticks in real-time.

It can be good to practice with this before actually entering trades and putting real money at risk. Just spend a few days closely watching a currency pair, and begin to identify the patterns seen in the candlesticks in real-time.

Another chart option that you can look at is called the relative strength index or RSI. This can be used in conjunction with your other tools. The purpose of this indicator is to tell you if there are "overbought" or "oversold" conditions. Overbought means that there has been too much buying and that the price is higher than it should be. When there are overbought conditions, chances are there is going to be a trend reversal.

Oversold is the opposite situation; there has been too much selling off of the asset. In the case of oversold conditions, too many people sold the asset off, and as a result, prices have gone down to levels that are lower than conditions really justify.

The value of the RSI will tell you if conditions are neutral, overbought, or oversold. If conditions are neutral, the RSI will be ranging between 20 and 80. If conditions are overbought, this is demonstrated by an RSI that is higher than 80. Finally, if conditions are oversold, this is demonstrated by an RSI that is lower than 20. These values are not fixed, however. Some traders who are more conservative use a narrower range, such as 30-70.

Just like other indicators, you should not use the RSI in isolation, or take action based solely on what the RSI is telling you. Let's take the case of a rising price trend. If the RSI is telling you that the asset is overbought, you see a crossing of the short-term moving average below the long-term moving average, and the candlesticks are indicating a trend reversal, this is a strong selling signal.

Now consider in a downtrend. If the RSI falls below 20 indicating that the asset is oversold, and you see the short-term moving average crossing above the long-term moving average, with signals of a trend reversal coming from the candlesticks, then you have evidence that is strong enough to take as a buying signal. So you can see that we will take multiple signals together, to confirm what we see in the candlesticks. If the candlestick patterns are not confirmed, then you might want to hold off on making a buying decision.

Drawing Trend lines

Drawing trend lines is a simple method that can be used to determine where pricing is going to end up, if the market appears to be moving strongly in one direction or the other. No matter which direction the price is moving, there are always going to be fluctuations. So let's consider a downward trend first. A part of the fluctuation is the fact that on the way down, there are always going to be peaks that occur, that is the asset will drop in price, then rise back up for a short time, then drop in price again, and repeat the process, with each peak as it rises up again getting smaller and smaller. This natural feature of declining prices makes it easy to estimate trends. Starting at the top peak, draw a straight line from the top of the peak, passing the line through all the peaks on the way downward. You want to extend the line past the current price so that you can get an estimate of future price levels, if the market continues to decline. This will be a downward sloping line.

If you are looking at an upward trend instead, you start at the first dip or trough in price. Then draw a straight line, with an upward slope, that connects the bottoms of all the dips on the way up to the right of the chart. This will allow you to get an estimate of where the price is heading if the trend continues.

Most trading platforms allow you to draw trend lines right on their charts on the screen, so you don't actually have to print out a chart and do this on a piece of paper, to estimate where the price is going. You will simply have to position the line in the right locations.

Chapter 6: Forex Trading Strategies

When you are trading a financial asset, you are going to have some wins, and you are going to have some losses. When you are a beginner, you might have more losses than wins if you don't put any time in to study how the markets work. Many beginners simply trade on the fly, going with their gut feelings. This is not a productive way to go about trading, and it can end up wiping out your account. When this happens, many traders simply give up and stop trading.

The goal of a trading strategy is to use proven methods to help you get more wins than losses. This can be combined with your knowledge of candlestick charts and what the indicators are telling you. It can also be combined with fundamental analysis. This is a term most frequently used in the stock markets, where fundamental analysis means studying the fundamentals of the company. That is, you go over their financial statements and look at things like how much debt the company is holding, what their inventories are and so forth. Then you look ahead by reading about the company's future plans and competition.

In the case of Forex markets, fundamental analysis is probably going to mean examining macro-economic factors. You are going to be checking how healthy a given economy is. You'll look at the GDP growth rates, the trends, and job creation numbers, for example. You are also going to want to look at the central bank policy, and what the current interest rates are. Trade and other factors are going to be important. Fundamental analysis will give you an overall idea of how strong a currency is relative to other currencies. However, fundamental analysis isn't really a strategy; it's more like another tool. So you can put it in the same category as candlesticks and indicators. If the fundamentals of a country are not good, that doesn't even mean you won't trade its currency. That can be a reason to bet on another country that is in a currency pair with the country that you are looking at.

There are many different trading strategies. One of the things that you will need to consider before trading is the time frame over which you want to operate. Many traders want to trade over very short time frames, taking smaller profits over short-term and usually smaller price moves. Others prefer to go long term, holding positions for days or even weeks (beware of interest rate risk).

There is no right or wrong answer to this question. So you have to try it, and possibly research it to determine what the best time frames are for you to use. This is a matter of personal style, and it's possible to make profits using any time frame. Some people find a longer time frame to be something that can generate a large amount of anxiety. The reason being that they are exposed to the position over long periods of time. Others find it more relaxing because currency pairs will naturally ebb and flow. This means that if you are willing to wait long enough, at some point, you are going to find an appropriate time to exit your trade and make a profit.

Day trading or holding a position for a few hours is not something that appeals to everyone either. If you are following a short-term trading strategy, one of the consequences of this is that you must pay close attention to the markets. You will have to be constantly checking to see how your investment is performing and look to the right time to exit the trade. And you will have to exit your trades very quickly. This can put a lot of stress on people, some are well-suited for it, but others may not be. In addition, it simply requires a commitment of time. Some people simply don't have the time to stare at their computer screens for hours on end. Of course, one advantage of the Forex market is that it runs 24 hours a day. This has major practical implications, and if you are too busy in the daytime because of a commitment to a job, you can do short-term trading strategies in the evening.

With that in mind, let's consider some of the main trading strategies that are used in the Forex markets.

Swing Trading

Swing trading is a simple idea to describe. If you are a swing trader, you will buy positions at the bottom of a downtrend. Then you will sell positions at the top of an uptrend. Of course, the trick is actually recognizing when the bottom of a downtrend or top of an uptrend actually occurs. This will require a solid knowledge of charting. You will watch a downtrend, and during this process be looking out for signals indicating a coming price reversal. When you see the signals, then you buy the currency pair.

Note that if you are talking about a currency pair A/B, you might have "sold" the currency pair in a bet on currency B rising against currency A. That means that in this case when you buy, you are actually exiting or closing your position.

But if you are betting on currency A, this is the point at which you enter the position.

Then you will ride the trend as long as you can. You can have an automatic order placed to exit when the price rises to a pre-determined level, or you can watch the charts for signals of a new trend reversal, that would take the currency pair A/B into a trend that is heading back down.

If you would prefer trading over a longer time period, swing trading is a trading style or strategy that might be to your liking. The idea behind swing trading is relatively simple. You look for price swings that take place over the course of days or weeks. Many Forex traders tend to be impatient, and if that is you, then you might not be suited for swing trading. As a swing trader, you are going to be required to hold your positions at least overnight. Some swing trades may involve holding a position for several weeks.

In some ways, swing trading is a more relaxed style of trading. You aren't sitting in front of your computer screen sweating bullets, waiting for the exact moment to exit the trade and take your profits. Instead, you might be checking the position only periodically.

However, swing trading cuts both ways. The Forex markets are highly volatile, and so this means that there are going to be a lot of short-term ups and downs. It requires a great deal of fortitude to wait these short-term price movements out. Some people actually find swing trading to be more stressful. For example, you might have bought the currency pair A/B, and so you are betting on A rising against B over a longer time frame. But you might see the price of the A/B pair drop considerably on its way to the higher price point. This is something that is important to be aware of because some people simply don't have the willpower to stick out a trade, when it appears to be going badly. But keep in mind that prices fluctuate all the time on Forex. It's unlikely that a price decline is going to be something that can be said to be a permanent thing. For the swing trader, it's a matter of simply waiting it out.

The biggest risk for swing trading might actually be the case of a price that doesn't move very much. We call this ranging. For simplicity, imagine that some financial security is trading at $1. We observe it over time and note that it fluctuates between $1 and $2. But it never goes above $2. Then, in that case, we call the $2 pricing level the resistance. It's resistant to further price increases at this time.

The lower price also forms a boundary. It is called support. That is a price that the asset can't break below for some reason.

If a financial asset is ranging, that doesn't mean you can't make a profit. You can buy the asset at the bottom or support level of the range, and simply wait for it to rise up to the resistance level, and then you can sell it for a relatively small profit.

If a financial asset is ranging, then you can get around this by purchasing a large quantity of the financial assets. Ranging is actually something that is suitable for swing trading, even if ranging is not going to be the ideal situation.

With swing trading, you are going to be looking for a breakout. This will require a close study of the candlestick charts, RSI, and moving averages. You are looking for signs of a big trend developing. This may mean having to track something else – the volume of trading.

If you see a trend reversal with a high volume of trading, this can be a good signal to get in your trade. Suppose that the trend has been dropping for some time. Then you see a moving average cross to the upside. You also note that oversold conditions exist, according to the RSI. A closer look reveals that the candlesticks are indicating a coming upward trend. This can be a good reason to open a position, and doing it with a buy order of a currency pair.

Then, as a swing trader, you will try and ride the trend as long as possible. Part of the strategy for a successful swing trader is having well-defined exit points. The first thing you will consider is the amount of loss you are willing to accept. You should not take this question lightly. On the one hand, you can limit the total losses that you are going to take on a trade. But on the other hand, asset prices often decrease, sometimes quite a bit, and then they reverse course. So it's more than possible for a losing trade to turn around and become a winning trade.

But you have to accept that sometimes you are going to be missing out on future profits. That is part of the trade-off that must be made, in order to have a successful business. You need to take profits, for sure. But you also need to protect yourself from losses. In order to protect yourself from losses in a somewhat automatic fashion, you can place what is called a stop-loss order. This is a limit order that you place to exit your position, if the price reaches a certain pricing point or beyond. A limit order means that the order is only going to execute if the market conditions meet the price set in your limit order. Speaking generally, if you are willing to take a $5 loss on a $50 financial asset, the limit order would be for an automatic sell order to be placed if the price of the asset dropped to $45.

This would protect our account from being wiped out on any single trade. Yes, we would take a hit and absorb some losses, but we would avoid being totally destroyed, and live to trade another day.

If you are interested in swing trading, you will also need to become acquainted with the concept of take profits. Essentially, this means that you put in a limit order to exit the position once a certain amount of profits are reached. Sometimes you will miss out on further gains, but setting up this sort of safety valve for your trading will ensure that you don't wait too long to get out of a position.

Even with the take profits order putting in a limit, one of the advantages of swing trading is that you are not going to be worried about spreads having an impact on your trading. The reason for this is that you will be able to look for large gains that will be larger than the spreads.

Within swing trading, there are several strategies that can be used to earn profits. We will explore those in the next chapter.

Scalping

Scalping is a totally different way to trade when compared to swing trading. If you have an idea what day trading is, it is entering and exiting a position on the same trading day. In Forex, scalping is an extreme form of day trading. The idea behind scalping is to enter and exit positions multiple times a day over short time periods, taking small profits with each trade. This works on Forex because it is a highly volatile market. At any given time, you can look for a new low price or high price, and then trade accordingly exiting the position when it does a "mini swing" in the opposite direction, if you are willing to only get a small profit off each trade. This is an approach to trading that is kind of like saving nickels and then adding them up to a million dollars over time. If scalping is your style, you are hoping to do a lot of trades. Scalping is actually pretty popular on the Forex markets.

Scalpers will use tick charts or trade on one-minute candlesticks. This is a very active form of trading, and you might have to trade 10 or more times per day to make significant profits. The goal for a scalper is to make small profits of 3-10 pips per trade. Your hope is that you are consistently making these small profits and that they will add up to big profits over long time periods.

Let's remember the size of a pip related to lot size. If you are talking about a micro lot, a pip is ten cents. So three pips are a mere 30 cents, and even ten pips are just a dollar. So scalping doesn't make too much sense for someone who is trading micro-lots. At the max end, you are only making a dollar per trade, and so you'd have to make 100 trades to make $100 a day, and that would be if all the trades produced the maximum amount of profit, something that is unlikely to happen.

With a mini lot, a pip is a dollar, so now you're looking at around $3, $5, and up to $10 profit per trade. It's easier to get to a significant amount of money at this level, but still very difficult.

It seems that to make significant profits scalping without having to do huge numbers of trades, you'd have to trade standard lots. Remember that in this case, a pip is $10, so if you make 5 pip profits that is $50, so you only have to do a few trades per day to make decent money. Even then, it's still going to be a rather active type of trading, and you are definitely looking at this being a full-time living. The less you make per trade, the more time you are going to have to devote to it, which almost ensures that you are going to have to trade standard lots, in order to make a living doing it.

Scalping is also going to involve having the get in and out of positions quickly. A 10-pip move can evaporate in a flash, and so if you get a 10-pip profit, you want to exit the trade immediately. That means you are going to have to select currency pairs that are going to be liquid. That way, you will be able to quickly close your position and take the profits that you are seeking.

Scalping is a high-risk strategy, and it's not for everyone.

Intraday Trading

Intraday trading is another day trading style, but it's more relaxed than scalping. So you are looking to enter and exit a position on the same trading day. However, rather than getting out of the position quickly, you're going to be doing fewer trades and looking for a larger amount of profit per trade. This will give you some flexibility to trade with smaller lot sizes, but you will probably have to trade multiple lots at a time. While a scalper is probably going to do 10 or 20 trades per day, you're going to be looking for larger profits in the 3-10 trade per day range.

Position Trading

If you are a position trader, you are willing to hold a position for a very long time (in Forex terms). That means you will hold the position at least for weeks, and you are willing to hold it for months, or even more than a year. Think of position trading as longer-term swing trading. The techniques are going to be about the same, but you are willing to wait long term in order to take the kind of profits that you are looking for. Position traders are not people who frequently trade, and they may spend a long time on the sidelines waiting for the right time to enter a position.

News Traders

Items in the news, including political, economic, and trade news, can have a big impact on currency prices. The impact is probably not going to be very long-lived in most cases, but while it's working, it can cause big price moves. These days with the 24-hour news cycle, there are always new controversies coming up that are going to increase volatility and send the markets going one way or another. A news trader seeks to follow the news and enter trades when this happens, and then ride the wave of the trend that gets created from the result. For example, the president may remark (or issue a tweet) that would cause the U.S. dollar to either rise in value or fall by a large amount. As soon as the tweet was issued, the news trader would enter positions that they think are going to move a large amount as a result of the remark. So if the remark were one that would probably lead to a rise in the dollar against the Euro, the news trader would sell Euro/USD currency pairs. Then they would use the techniques of chart analysis to look for a reversal after the trend takes on momentum, and exit the trade when the trend shows signs of beginning to reverse.

Trend trading

Many traders simply trade with the trend, when a long-term trend one way or the other can be identified. This is also a technique that can be used in conjunction with swing trading or position trading. The trick is accurately identifying trends that appear to be set up for a long ride upward or downward. This is called trading with the trend, or some traders say the trend is your friend. If you are trend trading, you have the luxury of being able to trade less liquid currency pairs, provided that the trend is stable. Of course, no trend is going to be stable forever, but it should be stable enough, so that you can ride the trend for a long period to earn profits and then remain in the trend for a time, when you try and exit the position. If you are looking at currency pairs that are not as liquid, getting out of the position is not going to be as easy, but you should be able to do it while still making good profits. Trend trading works with any lot size, and you can do fewer numbers of trades and seek larger profits per trade.

End of Day Trading

If you are an end of day trader, you are taking a more relaxed approach to trading, looking at the markets at the end of your day, and doing your technical analysis to enter or exit trades. This type of trading can be used within the context of other trading styles like swing trading and position trading, but of course, it's not going to be used with scalping or intraday trading. People who will retain a full-time commitment and don't have time to follow the markets all day long may use end of day trading. End of day is a figurative phrase, since Forex markets are open 24 hours, so it's a time of day that you pick in order to do your trades. You can do your analysis at this time, and determine which trades to enter or exit. The low-key aspect of this trading style makes it suitable for all lot sizes, and it does require some patience. You will have more flexibility and be able to wait for the size of profits you are hoping to take, and so you don't necessarily have to enter a large number of trades.

Chapter 7: Forex Trading Strategies – Techniques

In the last chapter, we described some of the general strategies that are used in forex trading. In this chapter, we are going to look at more specific strategies that could be used as part of one or more of the overall, or enveloping strategies described in the previous chapter. This is why I have also dubbed these as "techniques." None of the methods is necessarily linked to one specific strategy listed in the last chapter, although depending on whether you are a scalper or a swing trader (say) you will definitely have your preferences from this list.

Trendline Trading

Two chapters back, we described a procedure that involved drawing trendlines on your charts. This procedure can form the basis of a Forex strategy that can be used on any time frame that suits you. At a minimum, you need to have two dips for an upward trend or two peaks for a downward trend. Once you have drawn the trendline, you wait for the price to touch the trend line a third time. You can buy 2-5 pips above a high point or sell 2-5 pips below a low point.

CCI Moving Average Strategy

If you recall, we discussed RSI, which gives you information about overbought and oversold conditions. You can use the CCI oscillator for the same purpose. With a CCI moving average strategy, you will use two exponential moving averages together with the CCI oscillator. Typically, a 7-period exponential moving average and a 14-period exponential moving average are used. To enter a selling position, you look for a crossover, of the 7-period moving average to move below the 14-period moving average. Don't make a move immediately; you want to make sure that there is not going to be a rally that reverses the trend lines a second time. If the downtrend is confirmed, look for overbought conditions in the CCI. If you see overbought conditions, then it's a good time to sell a currency pair. For buying conditions, you will look for the formation of an upward trend. The first signal is going to be the 7-period exponential moving average crossing above the 14-period exponential average. Check the CCI for oversold conditions, and when you see that and confirm that there is not going to be a resumption of the downtrend, you buy your currency pair. This is good to use with the majors. You should also incorporate candlestick analysis to confirm your signals.

Bollinger Band Trading Strategy

Bollinger bands are a tool available on any trading platform. They provide you with a wealth of information, including a dynamic estimate of support and resistance. This is done using a 20-period moving average, which will display as the "middle" Bollinger band. The standard deviation, one above and one below (or many people use two standard deviation widths) form the upper and lower Bollinger bands. If the trend of the middle band is upward, then this is a buy signal. If the trend is downward, this is a selling signal. When you add Bollinger bands to a chart, you are going to see the price fluctuating about the middle Bollinger band, and going near (or slightly exceeding) the upper and lower Bollinger bands which mark out current levels of price support and resistance. To make a move, if the trend is upward and the price comes back and touches the middle Bollinger band, then buy your currency pair. On a downtrend, if the price rises back to touch the middle Bollinger band, then this is your sell signal.

Gartley Fibonacci Patterns

A Gartley pattern is a tool used to look for a retracement. This is when a temporary, and relatively small reversal happens before the overall trend resumes. What you want to look for as a pattern forming on the price chart that resembles the letter M. So the price will rise up, then drop down but not all the way down to the previous price level, rise up again, and drop down again. It's not going to be an ideal "M" shape, but instead, it will probably come up not quite as high on the second peak, and the last point is going to be higher than the first point on the far left. Wait for the pattern to appear on the chart. Then you want to check the candlestick patterns and see if there is a bullish reversal signal. Then you want to buy a currency pair at a price level that is 2 pips higher than the high price of the most recent bullish candlestick. To protect yourself in the event of a reversal, you can put a 5 pip stop loss order below the last closing price of the final bearish candlestick.

When using this technique to sell a currency pair, you look for the same setup but look for a bearish reversal pattern. Then you look to sell at 2 pips below the low price of the most recent bearish candlestick, and buy if the price goes 2-5 pips above the last high price seen in the chart.

The Floor Trader Strategy

The floor trading method is primarily a swing trading strategy, but it can be used for day trading as well. If you plan to use the floor trader strategy, you will rely on 9 periods, and 18-period exponential moving averages, and look for the 9-period moving average to cross below the 18-period moving average to signal a downtrend, and hence give a sell signal. Alternatively, you will look for the 9-period moving average to cross above the 18-period moving average to indicate an uptrend, which will be a signal to buy a currency pair. Then wait for a few candlesticks to pass to confirm that the trend is holding and that the candlesticks are showing no signs of reversal. Then you want to wait for a retracement before entering the trade. In a downtrend, this will allow you to sell at a relatively high price because a retracement is a temporary move upward in price before it resumes the longer-term downtrend.

Now let's consider the opposite situation. That is, we are going to look at an upward trend in price. This time, a retracement is doing to be a small drop in price before the trend resumes. So when the lines cross with the short-term moving average going above the long-term moving average, then you look for three candlesticks to go by to confirm that the trend is not going to reverse. Then wait for the retracement, and buy when the price dips to the relatively low.

The time frame depends on your time frame as a trader. So the candlesticks could be one-minute candlesticks if you are scalping, or 1 hour or even 1-day candlesticks if you are swing or position trading.

SuperTrends

Supertrend is an indicator that you can use on your charts, combining trend information with volatility data. Using this strategy, you will use two exponential moving averages. These will be the five-period exponential moving average, and the 20-period exponential moving average. As usual, you want to look for cross overs. When the five-period moving average crosses above the 20-period moving average, this is an indicator that an uptrend is coming.

Conversely, when the five-period moving average moves below the 20-period moving average, this tells us that a downtrend is coming. Then you want to combine this signal with the supertrend indicator. The supertrend indicator is going to be color-coded, either green or red. If it turns green and you see the five-period moving average crossing to the upside, this is a buying signal, so you will want to buy your currency pair at this point.

On the other hand, if the five-period moving average crosses below the 20-period moving average, and the super trend indicator turns red, this is a sell signal. Therefore, if you see this signal, then you will sell your currency pair. Super trends are very popular among Forex traders.

Hull Moving Average

The Hull moving average is a more sophisticated moving average. Like the exponential moving average, it uses price weighting to give more weight to recent prices when it computes the moving average. It is a surprisingly accurate moving average, and it will give you a nice smooth curve that seems to pass right through the centers of the candlesticks on your chart. If you want, you can use the Hull moving average in place of the exponential moving average for any strategy, but this type of strategy seems to work best when you are using one-day candlesticks. So it's going to be best suited for swing and position traders (or end of day traders as well) when looking for points to enter and exit your positions.

The strategy is the same as with other moving averages. That is, you are going to want to look for points, where a short period moving average crosses a moving average that has a longer period. If you are looking into a swing or position trading strategy, you are going to want to use longer periods. As an aside, when you use the longer periods the Hull moving average is not going to fit through the middles of the candlesticks, that happens for a nine period or less moving average.

For this case, using the Hull moving average for a longer time frame, you are going to want to set up a 50-period Hull moving average and an 80-period Hull moving average. The idea here is to look for the usual crossings and confirm by checking for reversal signals in the candlesticks.

Let's consider a buy signal first. Looking for a buy signal, there has been some sort of downtrend. You are keeping your eye open for the 50-period moving average to cross above the 80-period moving average.

When it does so, then you are going to want to look at the candlesticks. If you see an uptrend or bullish signal in your candlesticks, then this is a definite signal to buy a currency pair.

If you aren't sure about this, go back to the charting chapter and review the bullish signals given by candlesticks.

Now consider that the currency pair A/B has been in an uptrend. You may have either bought the currency pair A/B, and you are looking for the right time to close your trade by selling it. Alternatively, you could be looking for an opportunity to sell to open the A/B currency pair, so that you can bet on currency B against currency A.

The first thing you are going to look for is the crossing over of the lines. When you are in an uptrend, you should be seeing the short period moving average above the long-term moving average. When it crosses below, this is when you get ready to either close your position, if you had previously bought the A/B currency pair, or you are looking to sell to open. Either way, confirm the signal by checking the candlesticks. If it confirms that downtrend has been starting, then you can go ahead and make your move.

The Hull moving average method is not restricted to longer-term trading. You can use a shorter-term scenario with the Hull moving average. For example, if you are intraday trading, you could use a 9 period Hull moving average and a 20 period Hull moving average with 5-minute candlesticks.

Which Daily Routine Strategies to Use

There are many daily routine strategies for a Forex trader to choose from. The specific daily routine strategies used are not exclusive. So if you are trendline trading, that doesn't mean you couldn't also use other strategies. However, some people do tend to stick to one trading strategy, rather than mixing them up.

To get the best way forward, we need to go back to the last chapter. The first step in becoming an effective Forex trader is to focus on one and only one overarching strategy. By overarching strategy, I mean that you first focus on the main time frame that you are going to use for your trades. Are you going to be a scalper, an intraday trader, or a swing trader? This is the type of question that I am talking about in the present context. This is the first and most important question to settle in your mind.

Beginning traders should stick to one overarching strategy and one only. Later, when you get more experienced, you might want to try other methods. So you might start off using swing trading, and after you have a few months of experience under your belt, if you have the time available to do it, then you can consider trying out scalping at that time. In fact, many experienced traders are going to have one main style of trading they use, but they will dabble in other styles from time to time.

But beginning traders should stick to one style because you are going to end up with your head spinning around, if you try mastering multiple styles simultaneously. The best method for novices, in my humble opinion, is to use either end of day trading or swing trading. These trading methods do require a little bit of patience, but the advantage of these methods is that they are slower paced. If you try scalping, as a beginner it's going to be like being in a pressure cooker. This is going to cause you to make mistakes, and also you are going to get overwhelmed by emotions that will lead you to make many bad decisions. When we are talking about trading, we are talking about bad decisions leading to lost money.

So it's better to start off with a slower trading method that doesn't require you to be at your computer constantly, making split-second decisions. That type of trading style is best left for the experts. You can transition to that type of trading style after you have learned the methods through experience.

Now, what about the daily routine strategies considered in this chapter. It is true that some strategies might be better suited for one style or another. But the main thing behind these strategies is that they are actually pretty general in application. The main things we are looking for with the strategies is to spot a price reversal, which can give a buy or a sell signal. This can be done using all of the strategies listed here, except the trendline strategy.

While it's possible to pick and choose many strategies to use, it is probably better to stick to one or two strategies. First of all, any Forex trader needs to have a firm grasp on candlestick charts, and you need to be able to spot reversal patterns in the candlesticks on sight. So your first step in preparing to be a successful trader is to learn the candlesticks. There are many books and online courses that cover candlesticks in-depth, I suggest that you seek these out and really learn candlesticks from top to bottom.

The second tool that every Forex trader needs to understand and use are the moving averages. In fact, in the vast majority of cases, candlesticks and moving averages are all that you need. The specific moving average is not really that important. However, there is one exception here. Although simple moving averages are the default on some platforms, a price-weighted moving average is better to use for more accuracy. The exponential and Hull moving averages are quite effective for this purpose.

Trend line trading is more of an art than a science. It's also not something that takes a large amount of effort. As a result, traders that are using some of the strategies that are described in this chapter, are going to use trend line trading as well, at least some of the time. Generally speaking, trend line trading is something that will be used to give you an idea of where to go with your trades. It really cannot be considered as a technical indicator.

Novice traders are going to be intrigued and excited by all the various strategies. This can turn out to be a problem. It's better to master just a small set of strategies rather than trying to master them all. So look at all of them to try them out, then settle on just a couple that you will use over the long term. Here is a fact about the strategies. Many of them actually give you the same information. So there is no point in piling on different moving averages, for example.

Now a quick word about software products. There are many software products that are available on the market to do analysis and help you make your picks. Some software products will even suggest the currency pairs for you to trade. The software can automate all of the analysis that is done, and it will give you buy and sell signals. Since it can scan dozens of currency pairs in a matter of seconds or minutes, it can find currency pairs that are trending for you, so that you don't have to put time into doing this.

If you are going to use software tools, my advice is that you still put the time and effort in to learn how to read the charts, and how to spot reversals. You should not blindly trade based on what a software tool is telling you to do. What I suggest is that you confirm what the software tool is telling you to do, and if your mini-analysis agrees with the software, then you can buy or sell as indicated.

Chapter 8: Tips, Tricks, and Mistakes to Avoid

Now you have a grasp of the basics when it comes to Forex trading. We've explained what currency pairs are, and how you can buy and sell them to bet on different currencies against one another. We also looked into pips, and what that means along with different lot sizes. We talked about trading leverage. We introduced you to candlesticks and technical indicators, and investigated strategies that are often used by Forex traders.

So you are ready to go. But before you jump off the cliff and open a trading account, we are going to take a short look at some tips and tricks that will help you get off on the right foot as a novice trader. We will also look at some of the most common mistakes that novice traders make, and provide some suggestions that will help you avoid these common problems.

First of all, let me say upfront that the best traders are not going to be sloppy or careless people. They are going to be disciplined. That means they are going to put in a lot of time for preparation, and secondly, they are going to keep emotion out of the equation (see below). These two characteristics are the main things that separate good traders from bad traders.

Unfortunately, most traders are bad traders. The majority of Forex traders either barely make money, break-even, or they actually lose money while trading. But this is not a comment on the Forex markets at all. It's actually a comment about the traders themselves.

If you are serious and disciplined, and you take the time to put in preparation work, there is literally no reason why you can't make a living as a Forex trader. I will say upfront that right now, at this very moment that you are reading this book, the future as a Forex trader is going to be entirely up to you.

Planning, preparation, and careful thought are going to have to be ingredients that are part of your repertoire. If they are not, that means you are not going to find that you are a successful Forex trader. Remember one thing – despite its popularity – luck is not a factor in Forex trading. People think that it is, but people think that luck is a factor in everything. I will be completely honest with you here. It really is hard work and discipline that matters. Traders who try to rely on luck are the ones that fail. And luck certainly cannot explain why some traders make consistent profits, but others are trapped never getting anywhere. So don't give in to this mistaken attitude.

Train on a Demo Platform

If you're brand-new to trading, especially Forex trading, then you would really benefit from spending some time using a practice or demo platform. Many brokerages provide demo platforms that can be used to simulate trading. These demo platforms are actually pretty sophisticated. It's a full-throated simulation of the trading process and interface that the brokerages use. The advantage of this is that you will be able to go through the experience of placing trades and seeing how they play out. This will allow me to traders to test strategies and trading styles before actually putting any money down and putting the funds at risk. So in other words, you will be able to tell through the process of experience, which trading style is going to work best for you. Second, you will be able to train yourself by going through the experience of making mistakes. People often make mistakes of getting in or out of trades too early. People also panic and experience other emotions. Now one of the arguments against using demo platforms is that, since there is no real money involved, the emotions just aren't going to be there. That is certainly a valid argument. But it's not a valid argument that negates the benefits of training yourself using a demo platform.

While trading, the main benefit of using the demo platform is not really to explore the emotions that you will experience. Instead, the benefit is simply going through the process and seeing how the use of different strategies actually plays out. Of course, you could go back and look at some old data and do a kind of comparison. But that is not the same as actively going through the trade, following the trade, and seeing what really happens in the real world. The trading platform simulators, or demos, are so realistic that aside from actually putting real money, you're going to have a very hard time telling the difference between that and actual trade.

So one question the people ask is, how long should I spend using a demo platform? There is no firm answer to this question. I would certainly say that you should use a demo platform for at least a week and maybe even out to a month. Alternatively, you could use the demo platform for a couple of weeks, and then use it alongside the real platform, well only using small trades in your real account.

Ultimately, it's up to you. But one thing that we know is for sure, is that people who practice and put in a lot of hours of practice before they actually do an activity, tend to be the ones that end up as the experts in the field. This is true whether it is playing the violin, or trading on the Forex markets. I'm certain that all readers would agree that if you practice playing the violin for a month, if you were a total beginner, it's going to come out a lot better. We certainly wouldn't want to hear someone playing the violin that is playing for the very first time. But it's funny that people think that when it comes to something like trading Forex, they can just jump in and do it without having practiced. I know that doing this is not going to be all that exciting, then trust me; you will be better off if you take this approach.

Having a Trading Plan

One of the most important things of the trader needs to do is they need to develop a trading plan. Typically, most traders don't develop a trading plan. Instead what they do, is they trade on-the-fly. Now let's consider is what we talked about in the last section. I am sure that most readers are going to agree that the type of person that would scoff at using a demo platform for couple weeks to learn the basics of trading, is also going to be the same person that fails to develop a trading plan. Well, let's consider the following. Concerning determining your success or failure as a Forex trader, having a trading plan is going to be one of the most important factors. Simply put, having a trading plan is one of the most important things that you are going to need to get you a handle on when becoming a new Forex trader.

So what are some of the things that are going to go into Forex trading plan? The first item that you should, including your plan, is the balance you intend to keep in your Forex trading account. Keep in mind that when I say balance, I mean the total of cash plus positions held. So no matter what it is, let's say, $5000 or $10,000, pick a number to stick with for the next three months at least. Of course, if you find out that you are a successful Forex trader, you are going to want to increase the amount in your balance.

So having a balance enforces a bit of discipline with your account. First of all, if you end up taking some losses, you should stick to your plan and as soon as it's available deposit more money in the balance to bring it up to the level that you have determined. So if you set out and determine that you want to balance of $5000, and you take a loss, and your balance drops to $4000, stick to your plan and add another $1000 to the balance. However, in your first year of trading, I don't believe that you should add money to your account on a whim. You can reevaluate the situation every three months and adjust, as necessary. But for the three-month period, maintain the balance at the level that you have determined. The key point here is to avoid letting emotion drive you into pouring money into Forex trading out of excitement. Sometimes new traders get overwhelmed by excitement; maybe they've made a trade that is earning money. Amid their excitement, they might drain their bank account to fund more trades. And what happens more often than not is they end up getting into losing trades, because they are overexcited, and then they find themselves in a position where they have lost money.

So besides the amount of money that you're going to invest, let's take a look at some of the other things that we need to consider including a trading plan. The first thing that I would mention is you should have a goal for profits. At first, we aren't necessarily talking about actually meeting the goal. But you need to have a good idea of where you are going, so that you can take steps to correct your course, if you are not moving in the right direction. Second, your initial goals of profit should be modest. I know that many traders are anxious to get going, and they would love to drop their day job. But to have a realistic chance of doing that, unless you happen to be a whiz at trading, it's probably best to start off with small goals that you actually have a chance of meeting, and then each time you meet the goal, you can elevate to a new level.

So maybe you start small, like shooting for a profit of $500 over the course of a month. Once you meet the goal, you could raise the level. So using this example maybe after you have reached $500, then you change it to $1000. Over time, you'll find that soon enough you will be able to get in the situation where you are actually able to trade for a full-time living.

The next thing that we need to put in our trading plan, our fixed loss, and profit levels. This is going to be highly important for the purposes of enforcing discipline. It's only going to be up to you, so I can tell you what to do in order to be successful, but I can't be there with you when you make your trades. So some readers are going to read this and nod, but not follow the advice. If that's you, more than likely, you are not going to end up as a successful trader.

So you should take a level of profit that you are willing to accept and be happy about. This can be done in absolute terms, or it could be done in percentage terms. If we are talking about absolute terms, then you could set up a level of pips that you're willing to accept as a profitable move. Or as a percentage, you simply set the percentage gain or return on investment you're willing to accept with each trade. This is not something you are going to write down and then file away. Rather, you need to make this a rule that you follow with every single trade that you enter. Many platforms allow you to set up take profit levels with the trade. So you can use that feature and put a take profit order which is a limit order and then have it automatically executed. By the same token, you should figure out a maximum loss that you are willing to except on each trade. This can be done on a percentage basis. Then with every trade that you enter, you can enter a stop-loss order, so that it is automatically executed.

The next thing that should be included in your trading plan is a list of currency pairs you're going to focus on. In addition, your trading plan should include the main strategy that you're going to use for most of your trades.

Keep in mind that your trading plan does not have to be written in stone. But I would advise sticking to it for at least three months. So each quarter, you can revise the trading plan as you see fit. But then stick to it for three months, so that you can give it enough time to find out if it's working or not.

Trading Emotions

Emotion is one of the most important factors when it comes to trading, no matter what the type of financial asset is. More often than not, most traders who fail, whether it is day trading on the stock market, trading options, or trading on Forex, because they let emotions take over their decisions. This is one reason why having an automatic take profit and stop-loss orders is important. The first way that emotion interferes with the judgment of a trader is in the development of greed. This happens when you make a trade, and it suddenly starts going strongly in your favor. The problem with the greed is that it will put you in a position where are you are going to be staying in trades too long hoping to make a whole bunch of money. But what happens most of the time is that people fail to get out of the winning position, and they find out that it is turning into a losing position.

And of course, this works the other way as well. You can get overly emotional when you are losing money. As a result of this, traders panic, and they end up getting out of positions far too early. The fact of life when training in a highly volatile market is that prices are going to make wild swings up-and-down. Now, of course, you need to be protected against the case, when there is a catastrophic downfall in price. However, you also need to be prepared for a situation where the prices are going to dip down, and then it will rebound. This is where the problem comes in. Many traders panic when the price drops, and then they close all their positions. And then they go back and find out that the price actually moved back in their favor. So the bottom line is don't get emotional about your trading.

Conclusion

Forex trading is a very exciting trading market to become involved with. Trading Forex means fast-paced action, and the potential to profit by large amounts over short time periods. But remember that when you can win big, you can lose just as big. So while you are probably very excited about getting started with Forex trading, you should go slowly until you learn the methods.

This book should just be the start of your educational process. Although people are anxious to just jump in and get started with their trading, this is a bad approach. If you got excited about basketball and had no experience, would you show up to an NBA practice and expect to make the team?

Or if you suddenly got an interest in heart surgery, could you become a heart surgeon without going to medical school first?

Of course, these scenarios are ridiculous, and trading Forex is not heart surgery, or even playing in the NBA. But it's serious business. And it also involves real money. Despite this, people show up at the Forex markets, and they expect to be able to just start trading and making large profits without any preparation. You don't expect this in any other venture in life, so why would it work for Forex trading?

There aren't any formal schools to go to, so you are going to have to educate yourself. This will be a step-by-step process, and I sincerely hope that this book is only the beginning. It should open the doors for you so that you can approach more advanced and thorough treatments.

In addition to reading other books, consider taking some online courses. I don't advise paying thousands for a course —unfortunately, there are lots of hucksters out there on the internet that are eager to take your money just to teach you the basics you can find for free. Don't fall prey to that or to any claims that people can sell you picks. Instead, watch YouTube videos, or subscribe for low-cost Udemy courses that have high ratings.

Another way to train yourself, as you read more books and take courses, is to sign up for a demo account. Start practicing the methods and strategies but without using real money. This will give you experience, even though it's not "real." But it's like the NBA team, they practice before they play their first game. If you do the same, you will start out as a better trader.

Thank you for taking the time to read the book, and if you can, please drop by Amazon and leave a review for us.

Good luck trading!

www.ingramcontent.com/pod-product-compliance
Lightning Source LLC
Chambersburg PA
CBHW070654220526
45466CB00001B/436